SELECT LETTERS OF ST. AMBROSE

St. Ambrose of Milan

Translated by:

Henry de Romestin

Dalcassian
Publishing
Company

PHILADELPHIA, PA

STROMATA

Library of Congress Cataloging-in-Publication Data

STROMATA

STROMATA

LETTER XVII

This Epistle was written when Symmachus sent his memorial to Valentinian II. St. Ambrose presses on the Emperor the consideration that it is his business to defend religion, and not superstition. The memorial was sent without the adhesion of the Christian senators, and therefore did not represent that body. He warns Valentinian that if he accedes to the request he will incur the censures of the Church, besides acting in a manner derogatory to the memory of his father and brother.

Ambrose, Bishop, to the most blessed Prince and most Christian Emperor Valentinian.

1. As all men who live under the Roman sway engage in military service under you, the Emperors and Princes of the world, so too do you yourselves owe service to Almighty God and our holy faith. For salvation is not sure unless everyone worship in truth the true God, that is the God of the Christians, under Whose sway are all things; for He alone is the true God, Who is to be worshipped from the bottom of the heart; for the gods of the heathen, as Scripture says, are devils.

2. Now everyone is a soldier of this true God, and he who receives and worships Him in his inmost spirit, does not bring to His service dissimulation, or pretence, but earnest faith and devotion. And if, in fine, he does not attain to this, at least he ought not to give any countenance to the worship of idols and to profane ceremonies. For no one deceives God, to whom all things, even the hidden things of the heart, are manifest.

3. Since, then, most Christian Emperor, there is due from you to the true God both faith and zeal, care and devotion for the faith, I wonder how the hope has risen up to some, that you would feel it a duty to restore by your command altars to the gods of the heathen, and furnish the funds requisite for profane sacrifices; for whatsoever has long been claimed by either the imperial or the city treasury you will seem to give rather from your own funds, than to be restoring what is theirs.

4. And they are complaining of their losses, who never spared our blood, who destroyed the very buildings of the churches. And they petition you to grant them privileges, who by the last Julian law denied us the common right of speaking and teaching, and those privileges whereby Christians also have often been deceived; for by those privileges they endeavoured to ensnare some, partly through inadvertence, partly in order to escape the burden of public requirements; and, because all are not found to be brave, even under Christian princes, many have lapsed.

5. Had these things not been abolished I could prove that they ought to be done away by your authority; but since they have been forbidden and prohibited by many princes throughout nearly the whole world, and were abolished at Rome by Gratian of august memory, the brother of your Clemency, in consideration of the true faith, and rendered void by a rescript; do not, I pray you, either pluck up what has been established in accordance with the faith, nor rescind your brother's precepts. In civil matters if he established anything, no one thinks that it ought to be treated lightly, while a precept about religion is trodden under foot.

6. Let no one take advantage of your youth; if he be a heathen who demands this, it is not right that he should bind your mind with the bonds of his own superstition; but by his zeal he ought to teach and admonish you how to be zealous for the true faith, since he defends vain things with all the passion of truth. I myself advise you to defer to the merits of illustrious men, but undoubtedly God must be preferred to all.

7. If we have to consult concerning military affairs, the opinion of a man experienced in warfare should be waited for, and his counsel be followed; when the question concerns religion, think upon God. No one is injured because God is set before him. He keeps his own opinion. You do not compel a man against his will to worship what he dislikes. Let the same liberty be given to you, O Emperor, and let every one bear it with patience, if he cannot extort from the Emperor what he would take it ill if the Emperor desired to extort from him. A shuffling spirit is displeasing to the heathen themselves, for everyone ought freely to defend and maintain the faith and purpose of his own mind.

8. But if any, Christians in name, think that any such decree should be made, let not bare words mislead your mind, let not empty words deceive you. Whoever advises this, and whoever decrees it, sacrifices. But that one should sacrifice is more tolerable than that all should fall. Here the whole Senate of Christians is in danger.

9. If today any heathen Emperor should build an altar, which God forbid, to idols, and should compel Christians to come together there, in order to be among those who were sacrificing, so that the smoke and ashes from the altar, the sparks from the sacrilege, the smoke from the burning might choke the breath and throats of the faithful; and should give judgment in that court where members were compelled to vote after swearing at the altar of an idol (for they explain that an altar is so placed for this purpose, that every assembly should deliberate under its sanction, as they suppose, though the Senate is now made up with a majority of Christians), a Christian who was compelled with a choice such as this to come to the Senate, would consider it to be persecution, which often happens, for they are compelled to come together even by violence. Are these Christians, when you are Emperor, compelled to swear at a heathen altar? What is an oath, but a confession of the divine power of Him Whom you invoke as watcher over your good faith? When you are Emperor, this is sought and demanded, that you should command an altar to be built, and the cost of profane sacrifices to be granted.

10. But this cannot be decreed without sacrilege, wherefore I implore you not to decree or order it, nor to subscribe to any decrees of that sort. I, as a priest of Christ, call upon your faith, all of us bishops would have joined in calling upon you, were not the report so sudden and incredible, that any such thing had been either suggested in your council, or petitioned for by the Senate. But far be it from the Senate to have petitioned this, a few heathen are making use of the common name. For, nearly two years ago, when the same attempt was being made, holy Damasus, Bishop of the Roman Church, elected by the judgment of God, sent to me a memorial, which the Christian senators in great numbers put forth, protesting that they had given no such authority, that they did not agree with such requests of

the heathen, nor give consent to them, and they declared publicly and privately that they would not come to the Senate, if any such thing were decreed. Is it agreeable to the dignity of your, that is Christian, times, that Christian senators should be deprived of their dignity, in order that effect should be given to the profane will of the heathen? This memorial I sent to your Clemency's brother, and from it was plain that the Senate had made no order about the expenses of superstition.

11. But perhaps it may be said, why were they not before present in the Senate when those petitions were made? By not being present they sufficiently say what they wish, they said enough in what they said to the Emperor. And do we wonder if those persons deprive private persons at Rome of the liberty of resisting, who are unwilling that you should be free not to command what you do not approve, or to maintain your own opinion?

12. And so, remembering the legation lately entrusted to me, I call again upon your faith. I call upon your own feelings not to determine to answer according to this petition of the heathen, nor to attach to an answer of such a sort the sacrilege of your subscription. Refer to the father of your Piety, the Emperor Theodosius, whom you have been wont to consult in almost all matters of greater importance. Nothing is greater than religion, nothing more exalted than faith.

13. If it were a civil cause the right of reply would be reserved for the opposing party; it is a religious cause, and I the bishop make a claim. Let a copy of the memorial which has been sent be given me, that I may answer more fully, and then let your Clemency's father be consulted on the whole subject, and vouchsafe an answer. Certainly if anything else is decreed, we bishops cannot contentedly suffer it and take no notice; you indeed may come to the church, but will find either no priest there, or one who will resist you.

14. What will you answer a priest who says to you, The church does not seek your gifts, because you have adorned the heathen temples with gifts. The Altar of Christ rejects your gifts, because you have made an altar for idols, for the voice is yours, the hand is yours, the subscription is yours, the deed is yours. The Lord Jesus refuses and rejects your service, because you have served idols, for He said to you: 'You cannot serve two masters.' Matthew 6:24 The Virgins consecrated to God have no privileges from you, and do the Vestal Virgins claim them? Why do you ask for the priests of God, to whom you have preferred the profane petitions of the heathen? We cannot take up a share of the errors of others.

15. What will you answer to these words? That you who have fallen are but a boy? Every age is perfect in Christ, every age is full of God. No childhood is allowed in faith, for even children have confessed Christ against their persecutors with fearless mouth.

16. What will you answer your brother? Will he not say to you, I did not feel that I was overcome, because I left you as Emperor; I did not grieve at dying, because I had you as my heir; I did not mourn at leaving my imperial command, because I believed that my commands, especially those concerning divine religion, would

endure through all ages. I had set up these memorials of piety and virtue, I offered up these spoils gained from the world, these trophies of victory over the devil, these I offered up as gained from the enemy of all, and in them is eternal victory. What more could my enemy take away from me? You have abrogated my decrees, which so far he who took up arms against me did not do. Now do I receive a more terrible wound in that my decrees are condemned by my brother. My better part is endangered by you, that was but the death of my body, this of my reputation. Now is my power annulled, and what is harder, annulled by my own family, and that is annulled, which even my enemies spoke well of in me. If you consented of your own free will, you have condemned the faith which was mine; if you yielded unwillingly, you have betrayed your own. So, too, which is more serious, I am in danger in your person.

16. What will you answer your father also? Who with greater grief will address you, saying, You judged very ill of me, my son, when you supposed that I could have connived at the heathen. No one ever told me that there was an altar in the Roman Senate House, I never believed such wickedness as that the heathen sacrificed in the common assembly of Christians and heathen, that is to say that the Gentiles should insult the Christians who were present, and that Christians should be compelled against their will to be present at the sacrifices. Many and various crimes were committed while I was Emperor. I punished such as were detected; if any one then escaped notice, ought one to say that I approved of that of which no one informed me? You have judged very ill of me, if a foreign superstition and not my own faith preserved the empire.

17. Wherefore, O Emperor, since you see that if you decree anything of that kind, injury will be done, first to God, and then to your father and brother, I implore you to do that which you know will be profitable to your salvation before God.

LETTER XVIII

Reply of St. Ambrose to the Memorial of Symmachus, in which after complimenting Valentinian he deals with three points of the Memorial. He replies to his opponent's personification of Rome in a singularly telling manner, and proves that the famine spoken of by Symmachus had nothing to do with the cessation of heathen rites.

Ambrose, Bishop, to the most blessed prince and most gracious Emperor Valentianus, the august.

1. Since the illustrious Symmachus, Prefect of the city, has sent petition to your Grace that the altar, which was taken away from the Senate House of the city of Rome, should be restored to its place; and you, O Emperor, although still young in years and experience, yet a veteran in the power of faith, did not approve the prayer of the heathen, I presented a request the moment I heard of it, in which, though I stated such things as it seemed necessary to suggest, I requested that a copy of the Memorial might be given to me.

2. So, then, not being in doubt as to your faith, but anxiously considering the risk, and sure of a kindly consideration, I am replying in this document to the assertions of the Memorial, making this sole request, that you will not expect elegance of language but the force of facts. For, as the divine Scripture teaches, the tongue of wise and studious men is golden, which, gifted with glittering words and shining with the brilliancy of splendid utterance as if of some rich color, captivates the eyes of the mind with the appearance of beauty and dazzles with the sight. But this gold, if you consider it carefully, is of value outwardly but within is base metal. Ponder well, I pray you, and examine the sect of the heathen, their utterances, sound, weighty, and grand, but defend what is without capacity for truth. They speak of God and worship idols.

3. The illustrious Prefect of the city has in his Memorial set forth three propositions which he considers of force: that Rome, as he says, asks for her rites again, that pay be given to her priests and Vestal Virgins, and that a general famine followed upon the refusal of the priests' stipends.

4. In his first proposition Rome complains with sad and tearful words, asking, as he says, for the restoration of the rites of her ancient ceremonies. These sacred rites, he says, repulsed Hannibal from the walls, and the Senones from the Capitol. And so at the same time that the power of the sacred rites is proclaimed, their weakness is betrayed. So that Hannibal long insulted the Roman rites, and while the gods were fighting against him, arrived a conqueror at the very walls of the city. Why did they suffer themselves to be besieged, for whom their gods were fighting in arms?

5. And why should I say anything of the Senones, whose entrance into the inmost Capitol the remnant of the Romans could not have prevented, had not a goose by its frightened cackling betrayed them? See what sort of protectors the Roman temples have. Where was Jupiter at that time? Was he speaking in the goose?

6. But why should I deny that their sacred rites fought for the Romans? For Hannibal also worshipped the same gods. Let them choose then which they will. If these sacred rites conquered in the Romans, then they were overcome in the Carthaginians; if they triumphed in the Carthaginians, they certainly did not benefit the Romans.

7. Let, then, that invidious complaint of the Roman people come to an end. Rome has given no such charge. She speaks with other words. Why do you daily stain me with the useless blood of the harmless herd? Trophies of victory depend not on the entrails of the flocks, but on the strength of those who fight. I subdued the world by a different discipline. Camillus was my soldier, who slew those who had taken the Tarpeian rock, and brought back the standards taken from the Capitol; valour laid those low whom religion had not driven off. What shall I say of Attilius [Regulus], who gave the service of his death? Africanus found his triumphs not among the altars of the Capitol, but among the lines of Hannibal. Why do you bring forward the rites of our ancestors? I hate the rites of Neros. Why should I speak of the Emperors of two months, and the ends of rulers closely joined to their commencements. Or is it perchance a new thing for the barbarians to cross their boundaries? Were they, too, Christians in whose wretched and unprecedented cases, the one, a captive Emperor, and, under the other, the captive world made manifest that their rites which promised victory were false. Was there then no Altar of Victory? I mourn over my downfall, my old age is tinged with that shameful bloodshed. I do not blush to be converted with the whole world in my old age. It is undoubtedly true that no age is too late to learn. Let that old age blush which cannot amend itself. Not the old age of years is worthy of praise but that of character. There is no shame in passing to better things. This alone was common to me with the barbarians, that of old I knew not God. Your sacrifice is a rite of being sprinkled with the blood of beasts. Why do you seek the voice of God in dead animals? Come and learn on earth the heavenly warfare; we live here, but our warfare is there. Let God Himself, Who made me, teach me the mystery of heaven, not man, who knew not himself. Whom rather than God should I believe concerning God? How can I believe you, who confess that you know not what you worship?

8. By one road, says he, one cannot attain to so great a secret. What you know not, that we know by the voice of God. And what you seek by fancies, we have found out from the very Wisdom and Truth of God. Your ways, therefore, do not agree with ours. You implore peace for your gods from the Emperors, we ask for peace for the Emperors themselves from Christ. You worship the works of your own hands, we think it an offense that anything which can be made should be esteemed God. God wills not that He should be worshipped in stones. And, in fine, your philosophers themselves have ridiculed these things.

9. But if you deny Christ to be God, because you believe not that He died (for you are ignorant that death was of the body not of the Godhead, which has brought it to pass that now no one of those who believe dies), what is more thoughtless than you who honour with insult, and disparage with honour, for you consider a piece of wood to be your god. O worship full of insult! You believe not that Christ could die, O perversity founded on respect!

10. But, says he, let the altars be restored to the images, and their ornaments to the shrines. Let this demand be made of one who shares in their superstitions; a Christian Emperor has learned to honour the altar of Christ alone. Why do they exact of pious hands and faithful lips the ministry to their sacrilege? Let the voice of our Emperor utter the Name of Christ alone, and speak of Him only, Whom he is conscious of, for, the King's heart is in the hand of the Lord. Proverbs 21:1 Has any heathen Emperor raised an altar to Christ? While they demand the restoration of things which have been, by their own example they show us how great reverence Christian Emperors ought to pay to the religion which they follow, since heathen ones offered all to their superstitions.

11 *a*. We began long since, and now they follow those whom they excluded. We glory in yielding our blood, an expense moves them. We consider these things in the place of victories, they think them loss. Never did they confer on us a greater benefit than when they ordered Christians to be beaten and proscribed and slain. Religion made a reward of that which unbelief thought to be a punishment. See their greatness of soul! We have increased through loss, through want, through punishment; they do not believe that their rites can continue without contributions.

11. Let the Vestal Virgins, he says, retain their privileges. Let those speak thus, who are unable to believe that virginity can exist without reward, let those who do not trust virtue, encourage by gain. But how many virgins have the promised rewards gained for them? Hardly are seven Vestal Virgins received. See the whole number whom the fillets and chaplets for the head, the dye of the purple robes, the pomp of the litter surrounded by a company of attendants, the greatest privileges, immense profits, and a prescribed time of virginity have gathered together.

12. Let them lift up the eyes of soul and body, let them look upon a people of modesty, a people of purity, an assembly of virginity. Not fillets are the ornament of their heads, but a veil common in use but ennobled by chastity, the enticement of beauty not sought out but laid aside, none of those purple insignia, no delicious luxuries, but the practice of fasts, no privileges, no gains; all things, in fine, of such a kind that one would think them restrained from enjoyment while practising their duties. But while the duty is being practised the enjoyment of it is aroused. Chastity is increased by its own sacrifices. That is not virginity which is bought with a price, and not kept through a love of virtue; that is not purity which is bought by auction for money, which is bid for a time. The first victory of chastity is to conquer the desire of wealth, for the pursuit of gain is a temptation to modesty. Let us, however, lay down that bountiful provision should be granted to virgins. What an amount will overflow upon Christians! What treasury will supply such riches? Or if they think that gifts should be conferred on the Vestals alone, are they not ashamed that they who claimed the whole for themselves under heathen Emperors should think that we ought to have no common share under Christian Princes?

13. They complain, also, that public support is not considered due to their priests and ministers. What a storm of words has resounded on this point! But on the other hand even the inheritance of private property is denied us by recent laws, and no one complains; for we do not consider it an injury, because we grieve not at the

loss. If a priest seeks the privilege of declining the municipal burdens, he has to give up his ancestral and all other property. If the heathen suffered this how would they urge their complaint, that a priest must purchase the free time necessary for his ministry by the loss of all his patrimony, and buy the power to exercise his public ministry at the expense of all his private means; and, alleging his vigils for the public safety, must console himself with the reward of domestic want, because he has not sold a service but obtained a favour.

14. Compare the cases. You wish to excuse a decurio, when it is not allowed the Church to excuse a priest. Wills are written on behalf of ministers of the temples, no profane person is excepted, no one of the lowest condition, no one shamelessly immodest, the clergy alone are excluded from the common right, by whom alone common prayer is offered for all, and common service rendered, no legacies even of grave widows, no gifts are permitted. And where no fault can be found in the character, a penalty is notwithstanding imposed on the office. That which a Christian widow has bequeathed to the priests of a temple is valid, her legacy to the ministers of God is invalid. And I have related this not in order to complain, but that they may know what I do not complain of; for I prefer that we should be poorer in money than in grace.

15. But they say that what has been given or left to the Church has not been touched. Let them also state who has taken away gifts from the temples, which has been done to Christians. If these things had been done to the heathen the wrong would have been rather a requital than an injury. Is it now only at last that justice is alleged as a pretext, and a claim made for equity? Where was this feeling when, after plundering the goods of all Christians, they grudged them the very breath of life, and forbade them the use of that last burial nowhere denied to any dead? The sea restored those whom the heathen had thrown into it. This is the victory of faith, that they themselves now blame the acts of their ancestors whose deeds they condemn. But what reason is there in seeking benefits from those whose deeds they condemn?

16. No one, however, has denied gifts to the shrines, and legacies to the soothsayers, their land alone has been taken away, because they did not use religiously that which they claimed in right of religion. Why did they not practise what we did if they allege our example? The Church has no possessions of her own except the Faith. Hence are her returns, her increase. The possessions of the Church are the maintenance of the poor. Let them count up how many captives the temples have ransomed, what food they have contributed for the poor, to what exiles they have supplied the means of living. Their lands then have been taken away, not their rights.

17. See what was done, and a public famine avenged, as they say, the sad impiety that what was before profitable only for the comfort of the priests began to be profitable to the use of all. For this reason then, as they say, was the bark shipped from the copses, and fainting men's mouths supped up the unsavoury sap. For this reason changing grain for the Chaonian acorn, going back once more to the food of cattle and the nourishment of wretched provisions, they shook the oaks and solaced their dire hunger in the woods. These, forsooth, were new prodigies on

earth, which had never happened before, while heathen superstition was fervent throughout the world! When in truth before did the crop mock the prayers of the grasping husbandman with empty straw, and the blade of grain sought in the furrows fail the hope of the rustic crew?

18. And from what did the Greeks derive the oracles of their oaks except from their thinking that the support of their sylvan food was the gift of heavenly religion? For such do they believe to be the gifts of their gods. Who but heathen people worshipped the trees of Dodona, when they gave honour to the sorry food of the woodland? It is not likely that their gods in anger inflicted on them as a punishment that which they used when appeased to confer as a gift. And what justice would there be if, being grieved that support was refused to a few priests, they denied it to all, since the vengeance would be more unbearable than the fault? The cause, then, is not adequate to bring such suffering on a failing world, as that the full-grown hope of the year should perish suddenly while the crops were green.

19. And, certainly, many years ago the lights of the temples were taken away throughout the world; has it only now at length come into the mind of the gods of the heathen to avenge the injury? And did the Nile fail to overflow in its accustomed course, in order to avenge the losses of the priests of the city, while it did not avenge its own?

20. But let it be that they suppose that the injuries done to their gods were avenged in the past year. Why have they been unnoticed in the present year? For now neither do the country people feed upon torn up roots, nor seek refreshment from the berries of the wood, nor pluck its food from thorns, but joyful in their prosperous labours, while wondering at their harvest, made up for their fasting by the full accomplishment of their wishes; for the earth rendered her produce with interest.

21. Who, then, is so unused to human matters as to be astonished at the differences of years? And yet even last year we know that many provinces abounded with produce. What shall I say of the Gauls which were more productive than usual? The Pannonias sold grain which they had not sown, and Phætia Secunda experienced harm of her own fertility, for she who was wont to be safe in her scarcity, stirred up an enemy against herself by her fertility. The fruits of the autumn fed Liguria and the Venetias. So, then, the former year did not wither because of sacrilege, and the latter flourished with the fruits of faith. Let them too deny if they can that the vineyards abounded with an immense produce. And so we have both received a harvest with interest and possess the benefit of a more abundant vintage.

22. The last and most important point remains, whether, O Emperors, you ought to restore those helps which have profited you; for he says: 'Let them defend you, and be worshipped by us.' This it is, most faithful princes, which we cannot endure, that they should taunt us that they supplicate their gods in your names, and without your commands, commit an immense sacrilege, interpreting your shutting your eyes as consent. Let them have their guardians to themselves, let these, if they can,

protect their worshippers. For, if they are not able to help those by whom they are worshipped, how can they protect you by whom they are not worshipped?

23. But, he says, the rites of our ancestors ought to be retained. But what, seeing that all things have made progress towards what is better? The world itself, which at first was compacted of the germs of the elements throughout the void, in a yielding sphere, or was dark with the shapeless confusion of the work as yet without order, did it not afterwards receive (the distinction between sky, sea, and earth being established), the forms of things whereby it appears beautiful? The lands freed from the misty darkness wondered at the new sun. The day does not shine in the beginning, but as time proceeds, it is bright with increase of light, and grows warm with increase of heat.

24. The moon herself, by which in the prophetic oracles the Church is represented, when first rising again, she waxes to her monthly age, is hidden from us in darkness, and filling up her horns little by little, so completing them opposite to the sun, glows with the brightness of clear shining.

25. The earth in former times was without experience of being worked for fruits; afterwards when the careful husbandman began to lord it over the fields, and to clothe the shapeless soil with vines, it put off its wild disposition, being softened by domestic cultivation.

26. The first age of the year itself, which has tinged us with a likeness to itself as things begin to grow, as it goes on becomes springlike with flowers soon about to fall, and grows up to full age in fruits at the end.

27. We too, inexperienced in age, have an infancy of our senses, but changing as years go on, lay aside the rudiments of our faculties.

28. Let them say, then, that all things ought to have remained in their first beginnings, that the world covered with darkness is now displeasing, because it has brightened with the shining of the sun. And how much more pleasant is it to have dispelled the darkness of the mind than that of the body, and that the ray of faith should have shone than that of the sun. So, then, the primeval state of the world as of all things has passed away, that the venerable old age of hoary faith might follow. Let those whom this touches find fault with the harvest, because its abundance comes late; let them find fault with the vintage, because it is at the close of the year; let them find fault with the olive, because it is the latest of fruits.

29. So, then, our harvest is the faith of souls; the grace of the Church is the vintage of merits, which from the beginning of the world flourished in the Saints, but in the last age has spread itself over the people, that all might notice that the faith of Christ has entered minds which were not rude (for there is no crown of victory without an adversary), but the opinion being exploded which before prevailed, that which was true is rightly preferred.

30. If the old rites pleased, why did Rome also take up foreign ones? I pass over the ground hidden by costly building, and shepherds' cottages glittering with

degenerate gold. Why, that I may reply to the very matter which they complain of, have they eagerly received the images of captured cities, and conquered gods, and the foreign rites of alien superstition? Whence is the pattern for Cybele washing her chariots in a stream counterfeiting the Almo? Whence were the Phrygian bards, and the deities of unjust Carthage always hateful to the Romans? And her whom the Africans worship as Celestis, the Persians as Nitra, and the greater number as Venus, according to a difference of name, not a variety of deities. So they believed that Victory was a goddess, which is certainly a gift, not a power; is granted and does not rule, results from the aid of legions not the power of religions. Is that goddess then great whom the number of soldiers claims, or the event of battle gives?

31. They ask to have her altar erected in the Senate House of the city of Rome, that is where the majority who meet together are Christians! There are altars in all the temples, and an altar also in the temple of Victories. Since they take pleasure in numbers they celebrate their sacrifices everywhere. To claim a sacrifice on this one altar, what is it but to insult the Faith? Is it to be borne that a heathen should sacrifice and a Christian be present? Let them imbibe, he says, let them imbibe, even against their will, the smoke with their eyes, the music with their ears, the ashes with their throats, the incense with their nostrils, and let the dust stirred up from our hearths cover their faces though they detest it. Are not the baths, the colonnades, the streets filled with images sufficient for them? Shall there not be a common lot in that common assembly? The faithful portion of the senate will be bound by the voices of those that call upon the gods, by the oaths of those that swear by them. If they oppose they will seem to exhibit their falsehood, if they acquiesce, to acknowledge what is sacrilege.

32. Where, says he, shall we swear obedience to your Grace's laws and decrees? Does then your mind, which is contained in the laws, gain assent and bind to faithfulness by heathen ceremonies? The faith is attacked, not only of those who are present but also of those who are absent, and what is more, O Emperors, your faith, too, is attacked, for you compel if you command. Constantius of august memory, though not yet initiated in the sacred Mysteries, thought that he would be polluted if he saw that altar. He commanded it to be removed, he did not command it to be replaced. The removal has the authority of an act, the restoration has not that of a command.

33. Let no one flatter himself because he is absent. He who joins himself to others in mind is more present than he whose assent is given by bodily presence. For it is more to be united in mind than to be joined in body. The Senate has you as the presidents who convene the assembly, it comes together for you; it gives its conscience to you, not to the gods of the heathen; it prefers you to its children, but not to its faith. This is a love to be desired, this is a love greater than any dominion, if faith which preserves dominion be secure.

34. But perhaps it may move some that if this be so, a most faithful Emperor has been forsaken, as if forsooth the reward of merits were to be estimated by the transitory measure of things present. For what wise man is ignorant that human

affairs are ordered in a kind of round and cycle, for they have not always the same success, but their state varies and they suffer vicissitudes.

35. Whom have the Roman temples sent out more prosperous than Cneius Pompeius? Yet, when he had encompassed the earth with three triumphs, defeated in battle, a fugitive from war, and an exile beyond the bounds of his own empire, he fell by the hand of an eunuch of Canopus.

36. Whom has the whole land of the East given to the world more noble than Cyrus, king of the Persians? He too, after conquering the most powerful princes who opposed him, and retaining them, when conquered, as prisoners, perished, overthrown by the arms of a woman. And that king who was acknowledged to have treated even the vanquished with honour, had his head cut off, placed in a vessel full of blood, and was bidden to be satiated, being thus subject to the mocking of a woman's power. So in the course of that life of his like is not repaid by like, but far otherwise.

37. And whom do we find more devoted to sacrificing than Hamilcar, leader of the Carthaginians? Who, having offered sacrifice between the ranks during the whole time of the battle, when he saw that his side was conquered, threw himself into the fire which he was feeding, that he might extinguish even with his own body those fires which he had found to profit him nothing.

38. What, then, shall I say of Julian? Who, having credulously trusted the answers of the soothsayers, destroyed his own means of retreat. Therefore even in like cases there is not a like offense, for our promises have deceived no one.

39. I have answered those who provoked me as though I had not been provoked, for my object was to refute the Memorial, not to expose superstition. But let their very memorial make you, O Emperor, more careful. For after narrating of former princes, that the earlier of them practised the ceremonies of their fathers, and the later did not abolish them; and saying in addition that, if the religious practice of the older did not make a precedent, the connivance of the later ones did; it plainly showed what you owe, both to your faith, viz., that you should not follow the example of heathen rites, and to your affection, that you should not abolish the decrees of your brother. For if for their own side alone they have praised the connivance of those princes, who, though Christians, yet in no way abolished the heathen decrees, how much more ought you to defer to brotherly love, so that you, who ought to overlook some things even if you did not approve them in order not to detract from your brother's statutes, should now maintain what you judge to be in agreement both with your own faith, and the bond of brotherhood.

LETTER XX

St. Ambrose relates to his sister the events at Milan connected with the demand of the Arians for a basilica, and how the people rose up in opposition. Then that on the second day the basilica had been occupied by soldiers, who however fraternized with the Catholics. He gives a sketch of his address, comparing their trials to those of Job, more particularly those caused by his wife, and other cases owing to women. Though the basilica was surrendered, he himself had been threatened by a notary, but this did not trouble him. He adapts the story of Jonah to the present circumstances, relates the joy of the people at recovering their church, Valentinian's words to his courtiers, and the behaviour of Calligonus to himself. The date of the letter is Easter, a.d. 385.

1. Since in almost all your letters you enquire anxiously about the Church, you shall hear what is taking place. The day after I received your letter, in which you said you were troubled by dreams, the pressure of heavy troubles began to be felt. And this time it was not the Portian basilica, that is the one outside the walls, which was demanded, but the new basilica, that is the one within the walls, which is larger.

2. First of all some great men, counsellors of state, begged of me to give up the basilica, and to manage that the people should make no disturbance. I replied, of course, that the temple of God could not be surrendered by a Bishop.

3. On the following day this answer was approved by the people in the Church; and the Prefect came there, and began to persuade us to give up at least the Portian basilica, but the people clamoured against it. He then went away implying that he should report to the Emperor.

4. The day after, which was Sunday, after the lessons and the sermon, when the Catechumens were dismissed, I was teaching the creed to certain candidates in the baptistery of the basilica. There it was reported to me that they had sent decani from the palace, and were putting up hangings, and that part of the people were going there. I, however, remained at my ministrations, and began to celebrate mass.

5. Whilst offering the oblation, I heard that a certain Castulus, who, the Arians said, was a priest, had been seized by the people. Passers-by had come upon him in the streets. I began to weep bitterly, and to implore God in the oblation that He would come to our aid, and that no one's blood be shed in the Church's cause, or at least that it might be my blood shed for the benefit not of my people only, but also for the unbelievers themselves. Not to say more, I sent priests and deacons and rescued the man from violence.

6. Thereupon the heaviest sentences were decreed, first upon the whole body of merchants. And so during the holy days of the last week of Lent, when usually the bonds of debtors are loosed, chains were heard grating, were being placed on the necks of innocent persons, and two hundred pounds' weight of gold was required within three days' time. They replied that they would give as much or twice as much, if demanded, so that only they might preserve their faith. The prisons were full of trades-people.

7. All the officials of the palace, that is the recorders, the commissioners, the apparitors of the different magistrates, were commanded to keep away from what was going on, on the pretence that they were forbidden to take part in any sedition; many very heavy penalties were threatened against men of position, if they did not surrender the basilica. Persecution was raging, and had they but opened the floodgates, they seemed likely to break out into every kind of violence.

8. The Counts and Tribunes came and urged me to cause the basilica to be quickly surrendered, saying that the Emperor was exercising his rights since everything was under his power. I answered that if he asked of me what was mine, that is, my land, my money, or whatever of this kind was my own, I would not refuse it, although all that I have belonged to the poor, but that those things which are God's are not subject to the imperial power. If my patrimony is required, enter upon it, if my body, I will go at once. Do you wish to cast me into chains, or to give me to death? It will be a pleasure to me. I will not defend myself with throngs of people, nor will I cling to the altars and entreat for my life, but will more gladly be slain myself for the altars.

9. I was indeed struck with horror when I learned that armed men had been sent to take possession of the basilica, lest while the people were defending the basilica, there might be some slaughter which would tend to the injury of the whole city. I prayed that I might not survive the destruction of so great a city, or it might be of the whole of Italy. I feared the odium of shedding blood, I offered my own neck. Some Gothic tribunes were present, whom I accosted, and said, Have you received the gift of Roman rights in order to make yourselves disturbers of the public peace? Whither will you go, if things here are destroyed?

10. Then I was desired to restrain the people; I answered that it was in my power not to excite them; but in God's hands to quiet them. And that if they thought that I was urging them on, they ought at once to punish me, or that I ought to be sent to any desert part of the earth they chose. After I had said this, they departed, and I spent the whole day in the old basilica, and thence went home to sleep, that if any one wanted to carry me off he might find me ready.

11. Before day when I left the house the basilica was surrounded by soldiers. It is said that the soldiers had intimated to the Emperor that if he wished to go forth he could do so; that they would be in attendance, if they saw him go to join the Catholics; if not that they would go to the assembly which Ambrose had convened.

12. None of the Arians dared to go forth, for there was not one among the citizens, only a few of the royal family, and some of the Goths. And they as of old they made use of their waggons as dwellings, now make the Church their waggon. Wherever that woman goes, she carries with her all assemblage.

13. I heard that the Basilica was surrounded by the groaning of the people, but while the lessons were being read, I was informed that the new Basilica also was full of people, that the crowd seemed greater than when they were all free, and that a Reader was being called for. In short, the soldiers themselves who seemed to

have occupied the Basilica, when they knew that I had ordered that the people should abstain from communion with them, began to come to our assembly. When they saw this, the minds of the women were troubled, and one rushed forth. But the soldiers themselves said that they had come for prayer not for fighting. The people uttered some cries. With great moderation, with great instancy, with great faithfulness they begged that we would go to that Basilica. It was said, too, that the people in that Basilica were demanding my presence.

14. I then commenced the following address. You have heard, my children, the reading of the book of Job, which, according to the appointed order and season, is being gone through. By experience the devil also knew that this book would be explained, in which all the power of his temptations is shown and made clear, and so today he roused himself with greater vigour. But thanks be to our God, who has so established you with faith and patience. I had mounted the pulpit to praise Job alone, and I have found in you all Jobs to praise. In each of you Job lives again, in each the patience and valour of that saint has shone forth again. For what more resolute could have been said by Christian men, than what the Holy Spirit has today spoken in you? We request, O Augustus, we do not fight, we do not fear, but we request. This beseems Christians both to wish for peace and tranquillity, and not to suffer constancy of faith and truth to be checked by fear. For the Lord is our Leader, Who is the Saviour of them that hope in Him.

15. But let us come to the lessons before us. You see that permission is given to the devil, that the good may be tested. The evil one envies all progress in good, he tempts us in various way. He tried holy Job in his possessions, in his children, in pain of body. The stronger is tried in his own person, the weaker in that of another. And he was desirous of carrying off my riches which I possess in you, and wished to dissipate this patrimony of your tranquillity. And he strove to deprive me of yourselves also, my good children, for whom I daily renew the Sacrifice, you he endeavoured to involve in the ruin as it were of a public disturbance. I have then already been assailed by two kinds of temptation. And perhaps because the Lord our God knows me to be too weak, He has not yet given him power over my body. Though myself may desire it, though I offer myself, He deems me yet it may be unequal to this conflict, and exercises me with various labours. And Job did not begin with that conflict but finished with it.

16. But Job was tried by accumulated tidings of evils, he was also tried by his wife, who said, Speak a word against God and die. Job 2:9 You see what terrible things are of a sudden stirred up, the Goths, armed men, the heathen, the fines of the merchants, the sufferings of the Saints. You observe what was commanded, when the order was given surrender the Basilica; that is speak a word against God and die. And not only, speak against God, but, Do something against Him. For the command was, surrender the altars of God.

17. So, then, we are prepared by the imperial commands, but are strengthened by the words of Scripture, which replies: You have spoken as one of the foolish. That temptation then is no light one, for, we know that those temptations are more severe which arise through women. For even Adam Genesis 3:6 was overthrown by Eve, whereby it came to pass that he erred from the Divine commandments.

And when he recognized his error, feeling the reproach of a guilty conscience, he would fain have hidden himself, but he could not be hidden, and so God said to him: Adam, where are you? Genesis 3:9 that is, what were you before? Where have you now begun to be? Where had I placed you? Where have you wandered? You admit that you are naked because you have lost the robe of a good faith. Those are leaves with which you now seek to veil yourself. You have rejected the fruit, you desired to hide under the leaves of the Law, but you are betrayed. You have desired to depart from the Lord your God for the sake of one woman, therefore you flee from Him Whom you sought before to see. You have chosen to hide yourself with one woman, to forsake the Mirror of the world, the abode in Paradise, the grace of Christ.

18. Why should I relate that Jezebel, also persecuted Elisha after a bloodthirsty fashion? Or that Herodias Matthew 14:3 caused John the Baptist to be slain? Individuals persecuted individuals; but for me, whose merits are far inferior, the trials are all the harder. My strength is less, but I have more danger. Of women change follows on change, their hatreds alternate, their falsehoods vary, elders assemble together, wrong done to the Emperor is made a pretence. What is then the reason of such severe temptation against me, a mere worm; except that they are attacking not me but the Church?

19. At last the command was given: Surrender the Basilica. My reply was, it is not lawful for me to surrender it, nor advantageous for you, O Emperor, to receive it. By no right can you violate the house of a private person, and do you think that the House of God may be taken away? It is asserted that everything is lawful for the Emperor, that all things are his. My answer is: Do not, O Emperor, lay on yourself the burden of such a thought as that you have any imperial power over those things which belong to God. Exalt not yourself, but if you desire to reign long, submit yourself to God. It is written: The things which are God's to God, those which are Cæsar's to Cæsar. Matthew 22:21 The palaces belong to the Emperor, the churches to the Bishop. Authority is committed to you over public, not over sacred buildings. Again the Emperor was stated to have declared: I also ought to have one Basilica. My answer was: It is not lawful for you to have it. What have you to do with an adulteress? For she is an adulteress who is not joined to Christ in lawful wedlock.

20. Whilst I was treating on this matter, tidings were brought me that the royal hangings were taken down, and the Basilica filled with people, who were calling for my presence, so I at once turned my discourse to this, and said: How high and how deep are the oracles of the Holy Spirit! We said at Matins, as you, brethren, remember, and made the response with the greatest grief of mind: O God, the heathen have come into Your inheritance. And in very deed the heathen came, and even worse than the heathen came; for the Goths came, and men of different nations; they came with weapons and surrounded and occupied the Basilica. We in our ignorance of Your greatness mourned over this, but our want of foresight was in error.

21. The heathen have come, and in very truth have come into Your inheritance, for they who came as heathen have become Christians. Those who came to invade

Your inheritance, have been made coheirs with God. I have those as protectors whom I considered to be adversaries. That is fulfilled which the Prophet sang of the Lord Jesus that His dwelling is in peace, and There broke He the horns of the bows, the shield, the sword and the battle. For whose gift is this, whose work is this but Yours, Lord Jesus? You saw armed men coming to Your temple; on the one hand the people wailing and coming in throngs so as not to seem to surrender the Basilica of God, on the other hand the soldiers ordered to use violence. Death was before my eyes, lest madness should gain any footing while things were thus. You, O Lord, came between, and made of two one. Ephesians 2:15 You restrained the armed men, saying, If you run together to arms, if those shut up in My temple are troubled, what profit is there in My blood. Thanks then be unto You, O Christ. No ambassador, no messenger, but You, O Lord, have saved Your people, You have put off my sackcloth and girded me with gladness.

22. I said these things, wondering that the Emperor's mind could be softened by the zeal of the soldiers, the entreaties of the Counts, and the supplication of the people. Meanwhile I was told that a notary had been sent to me, to bring me orders. I retired a little, and he intimated the order to me. What were you thinking of, he said, in acting against the Emperor's decree? I replied: I do not know what has been decreed, and I have not been informed of what has been unadvisedly done. He asked: Why did you send priests to the Basilica? If you are a tyrant I wish to know it, that I may know how to prepare against you. I replied by saying that I had done nothing hastily regarding the Church. That at the time when I heard that the Basilica was occupied by soldiers, I only gave freer utterance to groans, and that when many were exhorting me to go there, I said: I cannot surrender the basilica, but I may not fight. But after I heard that the royal hangings had been taken away, when the people were urging me to go there, I sent some priests; that I would not go myself, but said, I believe in Christ that the Emperor himself will treat with us.

23. If these acts looked like tyranny, that I had arms, but only in the Name of Christ, that I had the power of offering my own body. Why, I said, did he delay to strike, if he thought me a tyrant? That by ancient right imperial power had been given by bishops, never assumed, and it was commonly said that emperors had desired the priesthood, rather than priests the imperial power. That Christ withdrew lest He should be made a king. That we had our own power; for the power of a bishop was his weakness. When I am weak, says the Apostle, then I become strong. 2 Corinthians 12:10 But let him against whom God has not stirred up an adversary beware lest he make a tyrant for himself. That Maximus did not say that I was the tyrant of Valentinian, he complained that by the intervention of my legation he had been unable to cross over into Italy. And I added that priests had never been tyrants, but had often suffered from them.

24. We passed that whole day in sadness, but the imperial hangings were cut by boys in derision. I could not return home, because the soldiers who were guarding the basilica were all around. We repeated Psalms with the brethren in the smaller basilica of the Church.

25. On the following day the Book of Jonah was read according to custom, after the completion of which I began this discourse. A book has been read, brethren, in which it is foretold that sinners shall be converted. Their acceptance takes place because that which is to happen is looked forward to at present. I added that the just man had been willing even to incur blame, in order not to see or denounce the destruction of the city. And because the sentence was mournful he was also saddened that the gourd had withered up. God too said to the prophet: Are you sad because of the gourd? and Jonah answered: I am sad. Jonah 4:9 And the Lord then said, that if he grieved that the gourd was withered, how much should He Himself care for the salvation of so many people. And therefore that He had put away the destruction which had been prepared for the whole city.

26. And without further delay, tidings are brought that the Emperor had commanded the soldiers to retire from the basilica, and that the sums which had been exacted of the merchants should be restored. How great then was the joy of the whole people! How just their applause! And how abundant their thanks! And it was the day on which the Lord was delivered up for us, on which penance is relaxed in the Church. The soldiers vied with each other in bringing in these tidings, rushing to the altars, giving kisses, the mark of peace. Then I recognized that God had smitten the early worm that the whole city might be preserved.

27. These things were done, and would that all was at an end! But the Emperor's words full of excitement foreshadow future and worse troubles. I am called a tyrant, and even more than a tyrant. For when the Counts were entreating the Emperor to go to the Church, and said that they were doing this at the request of the soldiers, he answered: If Ambrose bade you, you would deliver me up to him in chains. You can think what may be coming after these words. All shuddered when they heard them, but he has some by whom he is exasperated.

28. Lastly, too, Calligonus, the chief chamberlain, ventured to address me in peculiar language. Do you, said he, while I am alive treat Valentinian with contempt? I will take your head from you. My reply was, God grant you to fulfil your threat; for then I shall suffer as bishops do, you will act as do eunuchs. Would that God might turn them away from the Church, let them direct all their weapons against me, let them satisfy their thirst with my blood.

LETTER XXI

St. Ambrose excuses himself for not having gone to the consistory when summoned, on the ground that in matters of faith no one but bishops could rightly judge, and that he was not contumacious because he would not suffer wrong to be done to his own order. And he adds that Auxentius would perhaps choose as judges either Jews or unbelievers, that is, persons hostile to Christ. He says further that he is willing to discuss the matters in dispute at a synod, and that he would have told the Emperor by word of mouth what he is now writing, but that his fellow bishops and the people would not allow him to do so.

Ambrose, Bishop, to the most gracious Emperor and blessed Augustus, Valentinian.

1. Dalmatius, the tribune and notary, summoned me by the orders of your Clemency, as he asserted, demanding that I should also choose judges, as Auxentius had done. He did not mention the names of those who had been asked for, but he added that there was to be a discussion in the consistory, and that the judgment of your piety would give the decision.

2. To this I make, as I think, a suitable answer. No one ought to consider me contumacious when I affirm what your father of august memory not only replied by word of mouth, but also sanctioned by his laws, that, in a matter of faith, or any ecclesiastical ordinance, he should judge who was not unsuited by office, nor disqualified by equity, for these are the words of the rescript. That is, it was his desire that priests should judge concerning priests. Moreover, if a bishop were accused of other matters also, and a question of character was to be enquired into, it was also his will that this should be reserved for the judgment of bishops.

3. Who, then, has answered your Clemency contumaciously? He who desires that you should be like your father, or he that wishes you to be unlike him? Unless, perhaps, the judgment of so great an Emperor seems to any persons of small account, whose faith has been proved by the constancy of his profession, and his wisdom declared by the continual improvement of the State.

4. When have you heard, most gracious Emperor, that laymen gave judgment concerning a bishop in a matter of faith? Are we so prostrate through the flattery of some as to be unmindful of the rights of the priesthood, and do I think that I can entrust to others what God has given me? If a bishop is to be taught by a layman, what will follow? Let the layman argue, and the bishop listen, let the bishop learn of the layman. But undoubtedly, whether we go through the series of the holy Scriptures, or the times of old, who is there who can deny that, in a matter of faith — in a matter I say of faith — bishops are wont to judge of Christian emperors, not emperors of bishops.

5. You will, by the favour of God, attain to a riper age, and then you will judge what kind of bishop he is who subjects the rights of the priesthood to laymen. Your father, by the favour of God a man of riper age, used to say: It is not my business to judge between bishops. Your Clemency now says: I ought to judge. And he, though baptized in Christ, thought himself unequal to the burden of such a judgment, does your Clemency, who have yet to earn for yourself the sacrament of

baptism, arrogate to yourself a judgment concerning the faith, though ignorant of the sacrament of that faith?

6. I can leave it to be imagined what sort of judges he will have chosen, since he is afraid to publish their names. Let them simply come to the Church, if there are any to come; let them listen with the people, not for every one to sit as judge, but that each may examine his own disposition, and choose whom to follow. The matter is concerning the bishop of that Church: if the people hear him and think that he has the best of the argument, let them follow him, I shall not be jealous.

7. I omit to mention that the people have themselves already given their judgment. I am silent as to the fact that they demanded of your father him whom they now have. I am silent as to the promise of your father that if he who was chosen would undertake the bishopric there should be tranquillity. I acted on the faith of these promises.

8. But if he boasts himself of the approval of some foreigners, let him be bishop there from whence they are who think that he ought to receive the name of bishop. For I neither recognize him as a bishop, nor know I whence he comes.

4289. And how, O Emperor, are we to settle a matter on which you have already declared your judgment, and have even promulgated laws, so that it is not open to any one to judge otherwise? But when you laid down this law for others, you laid it down for yourself as well. For the Emperor is the first to keep the laws which he passes. Do you, then, wish me to try how those who are chosen as judges will either come, contrary to your decision, or at least excuse themselves, saying that they cannot act against so severe and so stringent a law of the Emperor?

10. But this would be the act of one contumacious, not of one who knew his position. See, O Emperor, you are already yourself partially rescinding your law, would that it were not partially but altogether! For I would not that your law should be set above the law of God. The law of God has taught us what to follow; human laws cannot teach us this. They usually extort a change from the fearful, but they cannot inspire faith.

11. Who, then, will there be, who when he reads that at one instant through so many provinces the order was given, that whoever acts against the Emperor shall be beheaded, that whoever does not give up the temple of God shall at once be put to death; who, say, is there who will be able either alone or with a few others to say to the Emperor: I do not approve of your law? Priests are not allowed to say this, are then laymen allowed? And shall he judge concerning the faith who either hopes for favour or is afraid of giving offense?

12. Lastly, shall I myself choose laymen for judges, who, if they upheld the truth of their faith, would be either proscribed or put to death, as that law passed concerning the faith decrees? Shall I then expose these men either to denial of the truth or to punishment?

13. Ambrose is not of sufficient importance to degrade the priesthood on his own account. The life of one is not of so much value as the dignity of all priests, by whose advice I gave those directions, when they intimated that there might perchance be some heathen or Jew chosen by Auxentius, to whom I should give a triumph over Christ, if I entrusted to him a judgment concerning Christ. What else pleases them but to hear of some insult to Christ? What else can please them unless (which God forbid) the Godhead of Christ should be denied? Plainly they agree well with the Arian who says that Christ is a creature, which also heathen and Jews most readily acknowledge.

14. This was decreed at the Synod of Ariminum, and rightly do I detest that council, following the rule of the Nicene Council, from which neither death nor the sword can detach me, which faith the father of your Clemency also, Theodosius, the most blessed Emperor, both approved and follows. The Gauls hold this faith, and Spain, and keep it with the pious confession of the Divine Spirit.

15. If anything has to be discussed I have learned to discuss it in church as those before me did. If a conference is to be held concerning the faith, there ought to be a gathering of Bishops, as was done under Constantine, the Prince of august memory, who did not promulgate any laws beforehand, but left the decision to the Bishops. This was done also under Constantius, Emperor of august memory, the heir of his father's dignity. But what began well ended otherwise, for the Bishops had at first subscribed an unadulterated confession of faith, but since some were desirous of deciding concerning the faith inside the palace, they managed that those decisions of the Bishops should be altered by fraud. But they immediately recalled this perverted decision, and certainly the larger number at Ariminum approved the faith of the Nicene Council and condemned the Arian propositions.

16. If Auxentius appeals to a synod, in order to discuss points concerning the faith (although it is not necessary that so many Bishops should be troubled for the sake of one man, who, even if he were an angel from heaven, ought not to be preferred to the peace of the Church), when I hear that a synod is gathering, I, too, will not be wanting. Repeal, then, the law if you wish for a disputation.

17. I would have come, O Emperor, to your consistory, and have made these remarks in your presence, if either the Bishops or the people had allowed me, but they said that matters concerning the faith ought to be treated in the church, in presence of the people.

18. And I wish, O Emperor, that you had not given sentence that I should go into banishment whither I would. I went out daily. No one guarded me. You ought to have appointed me a place wherever you would, for I offered myself for anything. But now the clergy say to me, "There is not much difference whether you voluntarily 429leave the altar of Christ or betray it, for if you leave it you will betray it."

19. And I wish it were clearly certain to me that the Church would by no means be given over to the Arians. I would then willingly offer myself to the will of your

piety. But if I only am guilty of disturbance, why is there a command to invade all other churches? I would it were established that no one should trouble the churches, and then I could wish that whatever sentence seems good should be pronounced concerning me.

20. Vouchsafe, then, O Emperor, to accept the reason for which I could not come to the consistory. I have never learned to appear in the consistory except on your behalf, and I am not able to dispute within the palace, who neither know nor wish to know the secrets of the palace.

21. I, Ambrose, Bishop, offer this memorial to the most gracious Emperor, and most blessed Augustus Valentinian.

LETTER XXII

St. Ambrose in a letter to his sister gives an account of the finding of the bodies of SS. Gervasius and Protasius, and of his addresses to the people on that occasion. Preaching from Psalm xix., he allegorically expounded the heavens to represent the martyrs and apostles, and the day he takes to be their confession. They were humbled by God, and then raised again. He then gives an account of the state in which their bodies were found, and of their translation to the basilica. In another address he speaks of the joy of the Catholics and the malice of the Arians who denied the miracles that were being wrought, as the Jews used to do, and points out that their faith is quite different from that of the martyrs, and that since the devils acknowledge the Trinity, and they do not, they are worse than the very devils themselves.

To the lady, his sister, dearer to him than his eyes and life, Ambrose Bishop.

1. As I do not wish anything which takes place here in your absence to escape the knowledge of your holiness, you must know that we have found some bodies of holy martyrs. For after I had dedicated the basilica, many, as it were, with one mouth began to address me, and said: Consecrate this as you did the Roman basilica. And I answered: Certainly I will if I find any relics of martyrs. And at once a kind of prophetic ardour seemed to enter my heart.

2. Why should I use many words? God favoured us, for even the clergy were afraid who were bidden to clear away the earth from the spot before the chancel screen of SS. Felix and Nabor. I found the fitting signs, and on bringing in some on whom hands were to be laid, the power of the holy martyrs became so manifest, that even while I was still silent, one was seized and thrown prostrate at the holy burial-place. We found two men of marvellous stature, such as those of ancient days. All the bones were perfect, and there was much blood. During the whole of those two days there was an enormous concourse of people. Briefly we arranged the whole in order, and as evening was now coming on transferred them to the basilica of Fausta, where watch was kept during the night, and some received the laying on of hands. On the following day we translated the relics to the basilica called Ambrosian. During the translation a blind man was healed. I addressed the people then as follows:

3. When I considered the immense and unprecedented numbers of you who are here gathered together, and the gifts of divine grace which have shone forth in the holy martyrs, I must confess that I felt myself unequal to this task, and that I could not express in words what we can scarcely conceive in our minds or take in with our eyes. But when the course of holy Scripture began to be read, the Holy Spirit Who spoke in the prophets granted me to utter something worthy of so great a gathering, of your expectations, and of the merits of the holy martyrs.

4. The heavens, it is said, declare the glory of God. When this Psalm is read, it occurs to one that not so much the material elements as the heavenly merits seem to offer praise worthy of God. And by the chance of this day's lessons it is made clear what heavens declare the glory of God. Look at the holy relics at my right hand and at my left, see men of heavenly conversation, behold the trophies of a heavenly mind. These are the heavens which declare the glory of God, these are His handiwork which the firmament proclaims. For not worldly enticements, but

the grace of the divine working, raised them to the firmament of the most sacred Passion, and long before by the testimony of their character and virtues bore witness of them, that they continued steadfast against the dangers of this world.

5. Paul was a heaven, when he said: Our conversation is in heaven. Philippians 3:20 James and John were heavens, and then were called sons of thunder; Mark 3:17 and John, being as it were a heaven, saw the Word with God. John 1:1 The Lord Jesus Himself was a heaven of perpetual light, when He was declaring the glory of God, that glory which no man had seen before. And therefore He said: No man has seen God at any time, except the only-begotten Son, Who is in the bosom of the Father, He has declared Him. John 1:17-18 If you seek for the handiwork of God, listen to Job when he says: The Spirit of God Who has made me. Job 33:4 And so strengthened against the temptations of the devil, he kept his footsteps constantly without offense. But let us go on to what follows.

6. Day, it is said, unto day utters speech. Behold the true days, where no darkness of night intervenes. Behold the days full of life and eternal brightness, which uttered the word of God, not in speech which passes away, but in their inmost heart, by constancy in confession, and perseverance in their witness.

7. Another Psalm which was read says: Who is like the Lord our God, Who dwells on high, and regards lowly things in heaven and in the earth? The Lord regarded indeed lowly things when He revealed to His Church the relics of the holy martyrs lying hidden under the unnoted turf, whose souls were in heaven, their bodies in the earth: raising the poor out of the dust, and lifting the needy from the mire, and you see how He has set them with the princes of His people. Whom are we to esteem as the princes of the people but the holy martyrs? Among whose number Protasius and Gervasius long unknown are now enrolled, who have caused the Church of Milan, barren of martyrs hitherto, now as the mother of many children, to rejoice in the distinctions and instances of her own sufferings.

8. Nor let this seem at variance with the true faith: Day unto day utters the word; soul unto soul, life unto life, resurrection unto resurrection; and night unto night shows knowledge; that is, flesh unto flesh, they, that is, whose passion has shown to all the true knowledge of the faith. Good are these nights, bright nights, not without stars: For as star differs from star in brightness, so too is the resurrection of the dead. 1 Corinthians 15:41

9. For not without reason do many call this the resurrection of the martyrs. I do not say whether they have risen for themselves, for us certainly the martyrs have risen. You know— nay, you have yourselves seen — that many are cleansed from evil spirits, that very many also, having touched with their hands the robe of the saints, are freed from those ailments which oppressed them; you see that the miracles of old time are renewed, when through the coming of the Lord Jesus grace was more largely shed forth upon the earth, and that many bodies are healed as it were by the shadow of the holy bodies. How many napkins are passed about! How many garments, laid upon the holy relics and endowed with healing power, are claimed! All are glad to touch even the outside thread, and whosoever touches will be made whole.

10. Thanks be to You, Lord Jesus, that at this time You have stirred up for us the spirits of the holy martyrs, when Your Church needs greater protection. Let all know what sort of champions I desire, who are able to defend, but desire not to attack. These have I gained for you, O holy people, such as may help all and injure none. Such defenders do I desire, such are the soldiers I have, that is, not soldiers of this world, but soldiers of Christ. I fear no ill-will on account of them, the more powerful their patronage is the greater safety is there in it. And I wish for their protection for those very persons who grudge them to me. Let them come, then, and see my attendants. I do not deny that I am surrounded by such arms: Some trust in chariots, and some in horses, but we will boast in the Name of the Lord our God.

11. The course of divine Scripture relates that Elisha, when surrounded by the army of the Syrians, told his servant, who was afraid, not to fear; for, said he, they that be for us are more than those against us; and in order to prove this, he prayed that the eyes of Gehazi might be opened, and when they were opened, he saw that numberless hosts of angels were present. And we, though we cannot see them, yet feel their presence. Our eyes were shut, so long as the bodies of the saints lay hidden. The Lord opened our eyes, and we saw the aids wherewith we have been often protected. We used not to see them, but yet we had them. And so, as though the Lord had said to us when trembling, See what great martyrs I have given you, so we with opened eyes behold the glory of the Lord, which is passed in the passion of the martyrs, and present in their working. We have escaped, brethren, no slight lead of shame; we had patrons and knew it not. We have found this one thing, in which we seem to excel those who have gone before us. That knowledge of the martyrs, which they lost, we have regained.

12. The glorious relics are taken out of an ignoble burying-place, the trophies are displayed under heaven. The tomb is wet with blood. The marks of the bloody triumph are present, the relics are found undisturbed in their order, the head separated from the body. Old men now repeat that they once heard the names of these martyrs and read their titles. The city which had carried off the martyrs of other places had lost her own. Though this be the gift of God, yet I cannot deny the favour which the Lord Jesus has granted to the time of my priesthood, and since I myself am not worthy to be a martyr, I have obtained these martyrs for you.

13. Let these triumphant victims be brought to the place where Christ is the victim. But He upon the altar, Who suffered for all; they beneath the altar, who were redeemed by His Passion. I had destined this place for myself, for it is fitting that the priest should rest there where he has been wont to offer, but I yield the right hand portion to the sacred victims; that place was due to the martyrs. Let us, then, deposit the sacred relics, and lay them up in a worthy resting-place, and let us celebrate the whole day with faithful devotion.

14. The people called out and demanded that the deposition of the martyrs should be postponed until the Lord's day, but at length it was agreed that it should take place the following day. On the following day again I preached to the people on this sort.

15. Yesterday I handled the verse, Day unto day utters speech, as my ability enabled me; today holy Scripture seems to me not only to have prophesied in former times, but even at the present. For when I behold your holy celebration continued day and night, the oracles of the prophet's song have declared that these days, yesterday and today, are the days of which it is most opportunely said: Day unto day utters speech; and these the nights of which it is most fittingly said that Night unto night shows knowledge. For what else but the Word of God have you during these two days uttered with inmost affection, and have proved yourselves to have the knowledge of the faith.

16. And they who usually do so have a grudge against this solemnity of yours; and since because of their envious disposition they cannot endure this solemnity, they hate the cause of it, and go so far in their madness as to deny the merits of the martyrs, whose deeds even the evil spirits confess. But this is not to be wondered at since such is the faithlessness of unbelievers that the confession of the devil is often more easy to endure. For the devil said: Jesus, Son of the living God, why are You come to torment us before the time? Matthew 8:29 And the Jews hearing this, even themselves denied Him to be the Son of God. And at this time you have heard the devils crying out, and confessing to the martyrs that they cannot bear their sufferings, and saying, Why are you come to torment us so severely? And the Arians say: These are not martyrs, and they cannot torment the devil, nor deliver any one, while the torments of the devils are proved by their own words, and the benefits of the martyrs are declared by the restoring of the healed, and the proof of those that are loosed.

17. They deny that the blind man received sight, but he denies not that he is healed. He says: I who could not see now see. He says: I ceased to be blind, and proves it by the fact. They deny the benefit, who are unable to deny the fact. The man is known: so long as he was well he was employed in the public service; his name is Severus, a butcher by trade. He had given up his occupation when this hindrance befell him. He calls for evidence those persons by whose kindness he was supported; he adduces those as able to affirm the truth of his visitation whom he had as witnesses of his blindness. He declares that when he touched the hem of the robe of the martyrs, wherewith the sacred relics were covered, his sight was restored.

18. Is not this like that which we read in the Gospel? For we praise the power of the same Author in each case, nor does it be a work or a gift, since He confers a gift in His works, and works in His gift. For that which He gave to others to be done, this His Name effects in the work of others. So we read in the Gospel, that the Jews, when they saw the gift of healing in the blind man, called for the testimony of his parents, and asked: How does your son see? when he said: Whereas I was blind, now I see. John 9:25 And in this case the man says, I was blind and now I see. Ask others if you do not believe me; ask strangers if you think his parents are in collusion with me. The obstinacy of these men is more hateful than that of the Jews, for the latter, when they doubted, at least asked his parents; the others enquire in secret and deny in public, incredulous not as to the work, but as to its Author.

19. But I ask what it is that they do not believe; is it whether any one can be aided by the martyrs? This is the same thing as not to believe Christ, for He Himself said: You shall do greater things than these. John 14:12 How? By those martyrs whose merits have been long efficacious, whose bodies were long since found? Here I ask, do they bear a grudge against me, or against the holy martyrs? If against me, are any miracles wrought by me? By my means or in my name? Why, then, grudge me what is not mine? If it be against the martyrs (for if they bear no grudge against me, it can only be against them), they show that the martyrs were of another faith than that which they believe. For otherwise they would not have any feeling against their works, did they not judge that they have not the faith which was in them, that faith established by the tradition of our forefathers, which the devils themselves cannot deny, but the Arians do.

21. We have today heard those on whom hands were laid say, that no one can be saved unless he believe in the Father, the Son, and the Holy Spirit; that he is dead and buried who denies the Holy Spirit, and believes not the almighty power of the Trinity. The devil confesses this, but the Arians refuse to do so. The devil says: Let him who denies the Godhead of the Holy Spirit be so tormented as himself was tormented by the martyrs.

22. I do not accept the devil's testimony but his confession. The devil spoke unwillingly, being compelled and tormented. That which wickedness suppresses, torture extracts. The devil yields to blows, and the Arians have not yet learned to yield. How great have been their sufferings, and yet, like Pharaoh, they are hardened by their calamities! The devil said, as we find it written: I know You Who You are, You are the Son of the living God. Mark 1:24 And the Jews said: We know not whence He is. John 9:30 The evil spirits said today, yesterday, and during the night, We know that you are martyrs. And the Arians say, We know not, we will not understand, we will not believe. The evil spirits say to the martyrs, You have come to destroy us. The Arians say, The torments of the devils are not real but fictitious and made-up tales. I have heard of many things being made up, but no one has ever been able to feign that he was an evil spirit. What is the meaning of the torment we see in those on whom hands are laid? What room is there here for fraud? What suspicion of pretence?

23. But I will not make use of the voice of evil spirits in support of the martyrs. Their holy sufferings are proved by the benefits they confer. These have persons to judge of them, namely, those who are cleansed, and witnesses, namely, those who are set free. That voice is better than that of devils, which the soundness of those utters who came infirm; better is the voice which blood sends forth, for blood has a loud voice reaching from earth to heaven. You have read how God said: Your brother's blood cries unto Me. Genesis 4:10 This blood cries by its color, the blood cries by the voice of its effects, the blood cries by the triumph of its passion. We have acceded to your request, and have postponed till today the deposition of the relics which was to have taken place yesterday.

LETTER XL

St. Ambrose begs Theodosius to listen to him, as he cannot be silent without great risk to both. He points out that Theodosius though God-fearing may be led astray, and points out that his decision respecting the restoration of the Jewish synagogue is full of peril, exposing the bishop to the danger of either acting against the truth or of death. The case of Julian is referred to, and the reasons given for the imperial rescript are met, especially by the plea that the Jews had burnt many churches. St. Ambrose touches on the temple of the Valentinians, whom he declares to be worse than heathen, and points out what a door would be opened to the calumnies of the Jews and a triumph over Christ Himself. The Emperor is lastly warned by the example of Maximus not to take the part of Jews or heretics, and is urged to clemency.

Ambrose, Bishop, to the most clement prince, and blessed Emperor, Theodosius the Augustus.

1. I am continually harassed by almost incessant cares, most blessed Emperor, but I have never been in such anxiety as at present, since I see that I must take heed that there be nothing which may be ascribed to me savouring even of sacrilege. And so I entreat you to listen with patience to what I say. For, if I am unworthy to be heard by you, I am unworthy to offer for you, who have been entrusted by you with your vows and prayers. Will you not yourself hear him whom you wish to be heard for you? Will you not hear him pleading his own cause whom you have heard for others? And do you not fear for your own decision, lest by thinking him unworthy to be heard by you, you make him unworthy to be heard for you?

2. But it is neither the part of an emperor to refuse liberty of speech, nor of a priest not to say what he thinks. For there is nothing in you emperors so popular and so estimable as to appreciate freedom in those even who are in subjection to you by military obedience. For this is the difference between good and bad princes, that the good love liberty, the bad slavery. And there is nothing in a priest so full of peril as regards God, or so base in the opinion of men, as not freely to declare what he thinks. For it is written: I spoke of Your testimonies before kings, and was not ashamed; and in another place: Son of man, I have set You a watchman unto the house of Israel, in order, it is said, that if the righteous does turn from his righteousness, and commit iniquity, because you have not given him warning, that is, hast not told him what to guard against, the memory of his righteousness shall not be retained, and I will require his blood at your hand. But if you warn the righteous that he sin not, and he does not sin, the righteous shall surely live because you have warned him, and you shall deliver your soul.

3. I had rather then, O Emperor, have fellowship with you in good than in evil, and therefore the silence of the priest ought to displease your Clemency, and his freedom to please you. For you are involved in the risk of my silence, but are aided by the benefit of my freedom. I am not, then, officiously intruding in things where I ought not, nor interfering in the affairs of others. I am obeying the commands of God. And I do this first of all out of love for you, good-will toward you, and desire of preserving your well-doing. If I am not believed in this, or am forbidden to act on this feeling, I speak in very truth for fear of offending God. For if my peril would set you free, I would patiently offer myself for you, though not willingly, for I had rather that without my peril you might be acceptable to God

and glorious. But if the guilt of silence and dissimulation on my part would both weigh me down and not set you free, I had rather that you should think me too importunate, than useless and base. Since it is written, as the holy Apostle Paul says, whose teaching you cannot controvert: Be instant, in season, out of season, reprove, entreat, rebuke with all patience and doctrine. 2 Timothy 4:2

4. We, then, also have One Whom it is even more perilous to displease, especially since even emperors are not displeased when every one discharges his own office, and you patiently listen to every one making suggestions in his own sphere, nay, you rebuke him if he act not according to the order of his service. Can this, then, seem to you offensive in priests, which you willingly accept from those who serve you; since we speak not what we wish, but what we are bidden? For you know the passage: When you shall stand before kings and rulers, take no thought what you shall speak, for it shall be given you in that hour what you shall speak; for it is not you that speak, but the Spirit of your Father Who speaks in you. Matthew 10:19-20 And if I were speaking in state causes, although justice must be observed even in them, I should not feel such dread if I were not listened to, but in the cause of God whom will you listen to, if not to the priest, at whose greater peril sin is committed? Who will dare to tell you the truth if the priest dare not?

5. I know that you are Godfearing, merciful, gentle, and calm, having the faith and fear of God at heart, but often some things escape our notice. Some have a zeal of God, but not according to knowledge. Romans 10:2 And I think that we ought to take care lest this also come upon faithful souls. I know your piety towards God, your lenity towards men, I myself am bound by the benefits of your favour. And therefore I fear the more, I am the more anxious; lest even you condemn me hereafter by your own judgment, because through my want of openness or my flattery you should not have avoided some fault. If I saw that you sinned against me, I ought not to keep silence, for it is written: If your brother sin against you, rebuke him at first, then chide him sharply before two or three witnesses. If he will not hear you, tell the Church. Shall I, then, keep silence in the cause of God? Let us, then, consider what I have to fear.

6. A report was made by the military Count of the East that a synagogue had been burnt, and that this was done at the instigation of the Bishop. You gave command that the others should be punished, and the synagogue be rebuilt by the Bishop himself. I do not urge that the Bishop's account ought to have been waited for, for priests are the calmers of disturbances, and anxious for peace, except when even they are moved by some offense against God, or insult to the Church. Let us suppose that that Bishop was too eager in the matter of burning the synagogue, and too timid at the judgment-seat, are not you afraid, O Emperor, lest he comply with your sentence, lest he fail in his faith?

7. Are you not also afraid, lest, which will happen, he oppose your Count with a refusal? He will then be obliged to make him either an apostate or a martyr, either of these alien to the times, either of them equivalent to persecution, if he be compelled either to apostatize or to undergo martyrdom. You see in what direction the issue of the matter inclines. If you think the Bishop firm, guard against making

a martyr of a firm man; if you think him vacillating, avoid causing the fall of one who is frail. For he has a heavy responsibility who has caused the weak to fall.

8. Having, then, thus stated the two sides of the matter, suppose that the said Bishop says that he himself kindled the fire, collected the crowd, gathered the people together, in order not to lose an opportunity of martyrdom, and instead of the weak to put forward a stronger athlete. O happy falsehood, whereby one gains for others acquittal, for himself grace! This it is, O Emperor, which I, too, have requested, that you would rather take vengeance on me, and if you consider this a crime, would attribute it to me. Why order judgment against one who is absent? You have the guilty man present, you hear his confession. I declare that I set fire to the synagogue, or at least that I ordered those who did it, that there might not be a place where Christ was denied. If it be objected to me that I did not set the synagogue on fire here, I answer, it began to be burnt by the judgment of God, and my work came to an end. And if the very truth be asked, I was the more slack because I did not expect that it would be punished. Why should I do that which as it was unavenged would also be without reward? These words hurt modesty but recall grace, lest that be done whereby an offense against God most High may be committed.

9. But let it be granted that no one will cite the Bishop to the performance of this task, for I have asked this of your Clemency, and although I have not yet read that this edict is revoked, let us notwithstanding assume that it is revoked. What if others more timid offer that the synagogue be restored at their cost; or that the Count, having found this previously determined, himself orders it to be rebuilt out of the funds of Christians? You, O Emperor, will have an apostate Count, and to him will you entrust the victorious standards? Will you entrust the labarum, consecrated as it is by the Name of Christ, to one who restores the synagogue which knows not Christ? Order the labarum to be carried into the synagogue, and let us see if they do not resist.

10. Shall, then, a place be made for the unbelief of the Jews out of the spoils of the Church, and shall the patrimony, which by the favour of Christ has been gained for Christians, be transferred to the treasuries of unbelievers? We read that of old temples were built for idols of the plunder taken from Cimbri, and the spoils of other enemies. Shall the Jews write this inscription on the front of their synagogue: The temple of impiety, erected from the plunder of Christians?

11. But, perhaps, the cause of discipline moves you, O Emperor. Which, then, is of greater importance, the show of discipline or the cause of religion? It is needful that judgment should yield to religion.

12. Have you not heard, O Emperor, how, when Julian had commanded that the temple of Jerusalem should be restored, those who were clearing the rubbish were consumed by fire? Will you not beware lest this happen now again? For you ought not to have commanded what Julian commanded.

13. But what is your motive? Is it because a public building of whatever kind has been burnt, or because it was a synagogue? If you are moved by the burning of a

building of no importance (for what could there be in so mean a town?), do you not remember, O Emperor, how many prefects' houses have been burnt at Rome, and no one inflicted punishment for it? And, in truth, if any emperor had desired to punish the deed sharply, he would have injured the cause of him who had suffered so great a loss. Which, then, is more fitting, that a fire in some part of the buildings of Callinicum, or of the city of Rome, should be punished, if indeed it were right at all? At Constantinople lately, the house of the bishop was burnt and your Clemency's son interceded with his father, praying that you would not avenge the insult offered to him, that is, to the son of the emperor, and the burning of the episcopal house. Do you not consider, O Emperor, that if you were to order this deed to be punished, he would again intervene against the punishment? That favour was, however, fittingly obtained by the son from the father, for it was worthy of him first to forgive the injury done to himself. That was a good division in the distribution of favour, that the son should be entreated for his own loss, the father for that of the son. Here there is nothing for you to keep back for your son. Take heed, then, lest you derogate anything from God.

14. There is, then, no adequate cause for such a commotion, that the people should be so severely punished for the burning of a building, and much less since it is the burning of a synagogue, a home of unbelief, a house of impiety, a receptacle of folly, which God Himself has condemned. For thus we read, where the Lord our God speaks by the mouth of the prophet Jeremiah: And I will do to this house, which is called by My Name, wherein you trust, and to the place which I gave to you and to your fathers, as I have done to Shiloh, and I will cast you forth from My sight, as I cast forth your brethren, the whole seed of Ephraim. And do not pray for that people, and do not ask mercy for them, and do not come near Me on their behalf, for I will not hear you. Or do you not see what they do in the cities of Judah? Jeremiah 7:14 God forbids intercession to be made for those.

15. And certainly, if I were pleading according to the law of nations, I could tell how many of the Church's basilicas the Jews burnt in the time of the Emperor Julian: two at Damascus, one of which is scarcely now repaired, and this at the cost of the Church, not of the Synagogue; the other basilica still is a rough mass of shapeless ruins. Basilicas were burnt at Gaza, Ascalon, Berytus, and in almost every place in those parts, and no one demanded punishment. And at Alexandria a basilica was burnt by heathen and Jews, which surpassed all the rest. The Church was not avenged, shall the Synagogue be so?

16. Shall, then, the burning of the temple of the Valentinians be also avenged? But what is but a temple in which is a gathering of heathen? Although the heathen invoke twelve gods, the Valentinians worship thirty-two Æons whom they call gods. And I have found out concerning these also that it is reported and ordered that some monks should be punished, who, when the Valentinians were stopping the road on which, according to custom and ancient use, they were singing psalms as they went to celebrate the festival of the Maccabees, enraged by their insolence, burnt their hurriedly-built temple in some country village.

17. How many have to offer themselves to such a choice, when they remember that in the time of Julian, he who threw down an altar, and disturbed a sacrifice,

was condemned by the judge and suffered martyrdom? And so the judge who heard him was never esteemed other than a prosecutor, for no one thought him worthy of being associated with, or of a kiss. And if he were not now dead, I should fear, O Emperor, that you would take vengeance on him, although he escaped not the vengeance of heaven, outliving his own heir.

18. But it is related that the judge was ordered to take cognizance of the matter, and that it was written that he ought not to have reported the deed, but to have punished it, and that the money chests which had been taken away should be demanded. I will omit other matters. The buildings of our churches were burnt by the Jews, and nothing was restored, nothing was asked back, nothing demanded. But what could the Synagogue have possessed in a far distant town, when the whole of what there is there is not much; there is nothing of value, and no abundance? And what then could the scheming Jews lose by the fire? These are artifices of the Jews who wish to calumniate us, that because of their complaints, an extraordinary military inquiry may be ordered, and a soldier sent, who will, perhaps, say what one said once here, O Emperor, before your accession: How will Christ be able to help us who fight for the Jews against Christ, who are sent to avenge the Jews? They have destroyed their own armies, and wish to destroy ours.

19. Further, into what calumnies will they not break out, who by false witness calumniated even Christ? Into what calumnies will not men break out who are liars, even in things belonging to God? Whom will they not say to have been the instigators of that sedition? Whom will they not assail, even of those whom they recognize not, that may gaze upon the numberless ranks of Christians in chains, that they may see the necks of the faithful people bowed in captivity, that the servants of God may be concealed in darkness, may be beheaded, given over to the fire, delivered to the mines, that their sufferings may not quickly pass away?

20. Will you give this triumph over the Church of God to the Jews? This trophy over Christ's people, this exultation, O Emperor, to the unbelievers? This rejoicing to the Synagogue, this sorrow to the Church? The people of the Jews will set this solemnity among their feast-days, and will doubtless number it among those on which they triumphed either over the Amorites, or the Canaanites, or were delivered from the hand of Pharaoh, King of Egypt, or of Nebuchodonosor, King of Babylon. They will add this solemnity, in memory of their having triumphed over the people of Christ.

21. And whereas they deny that they themselves are bound by the Roman laws, and repute those laws as criminal, yet now they think that they ought to be avenged, as it were, by the Roman laws. Where were those laws when they themselves set fire to the roofs of the sacred basilicas? If Julian did not avenge the Church because he was an apostate, will you, O Emperor, avenge the injury done to the Synagogue, because you are a Christian?

22. And what will Christ say to you afterwards? Do you not remember what He said by the prophet Nathan to holy David? I have chosen you the youngest of your brethren, and from a private man have made you emperor. I have placed of the fruit of your seed on the imperial throne. I have made barbarous nations subject

unto you, I have given you peace, I have delivered your enemy captive into your power. You had no grain for provision for your army, I opened to you the gates, I opened to you their stores by the hand of the enemies themselves. Your enemies gave to you their provisions which they had prepared for themselves. I troubled the counsels of your enemy, so that he made himself bare. I so fettered the usurper of the empire himself and bound his mind, that while he still had means of escape, yet with all belonging to him, as though for fear lest any should escape you, he shut himself in. His officer and forces on the other element, whom before I had scattered, that they might not join to fight against you, I brought together again to complete your victory. Your army, gathered together from many unsubdued nations, I bade keep faith, tranquillity, and concord as if of one nation. When there was the greatest danger lest the perfidious designs of the barbarians should penetrate the Alps, I conferred victory on you within the very wall of the Alps, that you might conquer without loss. Thus, then, I caused you to triumph over your enemy, and you give My enemies a triumph over My people.

23. Is it not on this account that Maximus was forsaken, who, before the days of the expedition, hearing that a synagogue had been burnt in Rome, had sent an edict to Rome, as if he were the upholder of public order? Wherefore the Christian people said, No good is in store for him. That king has become a Jew, we have heard of him as a defender of order, and Christ, Who died for sinners, soon tested him. If this was said of words, what will be said of punishment? And then at once he was overcome by the Franks and the Saxons, in Sicily, at Siscia, at Petavio, in a word everywhere. What has the believer in common with the unbeliever? The instances of his unbelief ought to be done away with together with the unbeliever himself. That which injured him, that wherein he who was conquered offended, the conqueror ought not to follow but to condemn.

24. I have, then, recounted these things not as to one who is ungrateful, but have enumerated them as rightly bestowed, in order that, warned by them, you, to whom more has been given, may love more. When Simon answered in these words the Lord Jesus said: You have judged rightly. Luke 7:43 And straightway turning to the woman who anointed His feet with ointment, setting forth a type of the Church, He said to Simon: Wherefore I say unto you, her sins which are many are forgiven, since she loved much. But he to whom less is forgiven loves less. Luke 7:47 This is the woman who entered into the house of the Pharisee, and cast off the Jew, but gained Christ. For the Church shut out the Synagogue, why is it now again attempted that in the servant of Christ the Synagogue should exclude the Church from the bosom of faith, from the house of Christ?

25. I have brought these matters together in this address, O Emperor, out of love and zeal for you. For I owe it to your kindnesses (whereby, at my request, you have liberated many from exile, from prison, from the extreme penalty of death) that I should not fear even offending your feelings for the sake of your own salvation (no one has greater confidence than he who loves from his heart, certainly no one ought to injure him who takes thought for him); that I may not lose in one moment that favour granted to every priest and received by me for so many years; and yet it is not the loss of favour which I deprecate but the peril to salvation.

26. And yet how great a thing it is, O Emperor, that you should not think it necessary to enquire or to punish in regard to a matter as to which up to this day no one has enquired, no one has ever inflicted punishment. It is a serious matter to endanger your salvation for the Jews. When Gideon had slain the sacred calf, the heathen said, The gods will themselves avenge the injury done to them. Who is to avenge the Synagogue? Christ, Whom they slew, Whom they denied? Will God the Father avenge those who do not receive the Father, since they have not received the Son? Who is to avenge the heresy of the Valentinians? How can your piety avenge them, seeing it has commanded them to be excluded, and denied them permission to meet together? If I set before you Josiah as a king approved of God, will you condemn that in them which was approved in him?

27. But at any rate if too little confidence is placed in me, command the presence of those bishops whom you think fit, let it be discussed, O Emperor, what ought to be done without injury to the faith. If you consult your officers concerning pecuniary causes, how much more just is it that you should consult the priests of God in the cause of religion.

28. Let your Clemency consider from how many plotters, how many spies the Church suffers. If they come upon a slight crack, they plant a dart in it. I speak after the manner of men, but God is feared more than men, Who is rightly set before even emperors. If any one thinks it right that deference should be paid to a friend, a parent, or a neighbour, I am right in judging that deference should be paid to God, and that He should be preferred to all. Consult, O Emperor, your own advantage, or suffer me to consult mine.

29. What shall I answer hereafter, if it be discovered that, by authority given from this place, Christians have been slain by the sword, or by clubs, or thongs knotted with lead? How shall I explain such a fact? How shall I excuse it to those bishops, who now mourn bitterly because some, who have discharged the office of the priesthood for thirty and many more years, or other ministers of the Church, are withdrawn from their sacred office, and set to discharge municipal duties? For if they who war for you serve for a stated time of service, how much more ought you to consider those who war for God. How, I say, shall I excuse this to the bishops, who make complaint concerning the clergy, and write that the Churches are wasted by a serious attack upon them?

30. I was desirous that this should come to the knowledge of your Clemency. You will, when it pleases you, vouchsafe to consider and give order according to your will, but exclude and cast out that which troubles me, and troubles me rightly. You do yourself whatever you order to be done, even if he, your officer, do not do it. I much prefer that you should be merciful, than that he should not do what he has been ordered.

31. You have those for whom you ought yet to invite and to merit the mercy of the Lord in regard to the Roman Empire; you have those for whom you hope even more than for yourself; let the grace of God for them, let their salvation appeal to you in these words of mine. I fear that you may commit your cause to the judgment of others. Everything is still unprejudiced before you. On this point I

pledge myself to our God for you, do not fear your oath. Is it possible that that should displease God which is amended for His honour? You need not alter anything in that letter, whether it be sent or is not yet sent. Order another to be written, which shall be full of faith, full of piety. For you it is possible to change for the better, for me it is not possible to hide the truth.

32. You forgave the Antiochians the insult offered to you; you have recalled the daughters of your enemy, and given them to be brought up by a relative; you sent sums of money to the mother of your enemy from your own treasury. This so great piety, this so great faith towards God, will be darkened by this deed. Do not you, then, I entreat, who spared enemies in arms, and preserved your adversaries, think that Christians ought to be punished with such eagerness.

33. And now, O Emperor, I beg you not to disdain to hear me who am in fear both for yourself and for myself, for it is the voice of a Saint which says: Wherefore was I made to see the misery of my people? 1 Maccabbees 2:7 that I should commit an offense against God. I, indeed, have done what could be done consistently with honour to you, that you might rather listen to me in the palace, lest, if it were necessary, you should listen to me in the Church.

LETTER XLI

St. Ambrose in this letter to his sister continues the account of the matters contained in his letter to Theodosius, and of a sermon which he subsequently delivered before the Emperor, with the result that the Emperor, when St. Ambrose refused to offer the Sacrifice before receiving a promise that the objectionable order should be revoked, yielded.

The Brother to His Sister.

1. You were good enough to write me word that your holiness was still anxious, because I had written that I was so, so that I am surprised that you did not receive my letter in which I wrote word that satisfaction had been granted me. For when it was reported that a synagogue of the Jews and a conventicle of the Valentinians had been burnt by Christians at the instigation of the bishop, an order was made while I was at Aquileia, that the synagogue should be rebuilt, and the monks punished who had burnt the Valentinian building. Then since I gained little by frequent endeavours, I wrote and sent a letter to the Emperor, and when he went to church I delivered this discourse.

2. In the book of the prophet it is written: Take to yourself the rod of an almond tree. Jeremiah 1:11 We ought to consider why the Lord said this to the prophet, for it was not written without a purpose, since in the Pentateuch too we read that the almond rod of Aaron the priest, after being long laid up, blossomed. For the Lord seems to signify by the rod that the prophetic or priestly authority ought to be straightforward, and to advise not so much what is pleasant as what is expedient.

3. And so the prophet is bidden to take an almond rod, because the fruit of this tree is bitter in its rind, hard in its shell, and inside it is pleasant, that after its likeness the prophet should set forth things bitter and hard, and should not fear to proclaim harsh things. Likewise also the priest; for his teaching, though for a time it may seem bitter to some, and like Aaron's rod be long laid up in the ears of dissemblers, yet after a time, when it is thought to have dried up, it blossoms.

4. Wherefore also the Apostle says: What will you, shall I come to you with a rod, or in love and in the spirit of gentleness? 1 Corinthians 4:21 First he made mention of the rod, and like the almond rod struck those who were wandering, that he might afterwards comfort them in the spirit of meekness. And so meekness restored him whom the rod had deprived of the heavenly sacraments. And to his disciple he gave similar injunctions, saying: Reprove, beseech, rebuke. 2 Corinthians 2:10 Two of these are hard, one is gentle, but they are hard only that they may soften; for as to suffering from excess of gall, bitter food or drink seems sweet, and on the other hand sweet food is bitter, so where the mind is wounded it grows worse under the influence of pleasurable flattery, and again is made sound by the bitterness of correction.

5. Let thus much be gathered from the passage of the prophet, and let us now consider what the lesson from the Gospel contains: One of the Pharisees invited the Lord Jesus to eat with him, and He entered into the Pharisee's house and sat down. And behold a woman, who was a sinner in the city, when she knew that

Jesus sat at meat in the Pharisee's house, brought an alabaster box of ointment, and standing behind at His feet, began to wash His feet with her tears. And then he read as far as this place: Your faith has saved you, go in peace. How simple, I went on to say, is this Gospel lesson in words, how deep in its counsels! And so because the words are those of the Great Counsellor, Isaiah 9:6 let us consider their depth.

6. Our Lord Jesus Christ judged that men could more readily be bound and led on to do the things that are right by kindness than by fear, and that love avails more than dread for correction. And so, when He came, being born of a Virgin, He sent forth His grace, that sin might be forgiven in baptism in order to make us more grateful to Himself. Then if we repay Him by services befitting men who are grateful, He has declared in this woman that there will be a reward for this grace itself to all men. For if He had forgiven only our original debt, He would have seemed more cautious than merciful, and more careful for our correction than magnificent in His rewards. It is only the cunning of a narrow mind that tries to entice, but it is fitting for God that those whom He has invited by grace He should lead on by increase of that grace. And so He first bestows on us a gift by baptism, and afterwards gives more abundantly to those who serve Him faithfully. So, then, the benefits of Christ are both incentives and rewards of virtue.

7. And let no one be startled at the word creditor. Luke 7:41 We were before under a hard creditor, who was not to be satisfied and paid to the full but by the death of the debtor. The Lord Jesus came, He saw us bound by a heavy debt. No one could pay his debt with the patrimony of his innocence. I could have nothing of my own wherewith to free myself. He gave to me a new kind of acquittance, changing my creditor because I had nothing wherewith to pay my debt. But it was sin, not nature, which had made us debtors, for we had contracted heavy debts by our sins, that we who had been free should be bound, for he is a debtor who received any of his creditor's money. Now sin is of the devil; that wicked one has, as it were, these riches in his possession. For as the riches of Christ are virtues, so crimes are the wealth of the devil. He had reduced the human race to perpetual captivity by the heavy debt of inherited liability, which our debt-laden ancestor had transmitted to his posterity by inheritance. The Lord Jesus came, He offered His death for the death of all, He poured out His Blood for the blood of all.

8. So, then, we have changed our creditor, not escaped wholly, or rather we have escaped, for the debt remains but the interest is cancelled, for the Lord Jesus said, To those who are in bonds, Come out, and to those who are in prison, Go forth; Isaiah 49:9 so your sins are forgiven. All, then, are forgiven, nor is there any one whom He has not loosed. For thus it is written, that He has forgiven all transgressions, doing away the handwriting of the ordinance that was against us. Colossians 2:13-14 Why, then, do we hold the bonds of others, and desire to exact the debts of others, while we enjoy our own remission? He who forgave all, required of all that what every one remembers to have been forgiven to himself, he also should forgive others.

9. Take care that you do not begin to be in a worse case as creditor than as debtor, like the man in the Gospel, to whom his lord forgave all his debt, and who

afterwards began to exact from his fellow-servant that which he himself had not paid, for which reason his master being angry, exacted from him, with the bitterest reproaches, that which he had before forgiven him. Let us, therefore, take heed lest this happen to us, that by not forgiving that which is due to ourselves, we should incur the payment of what has been forgiven us, for thus is it written in the words of the Lord Jesus: So shall My Father, Which is in heaven, do also unto you, if you from your hearts forgive not every one his brother. Matthew 18:35 Let us, then, forgive few things to whom many have been forgiven, and understand that the more we forgive the more acceptable shall we be to God, for we are the more well pleasing to God, the more we have been forgiven.

10. And, finally, the Pharisee, when the Lord asked him, which of them loved him most, Luke 7:42 answered, I suppose that he to whom he forgave most. And the Lord replied, You have judged rightly. Luke 7:43 The judgment of the Pharisee is praised, but his affection is blamed. He judges well concerning others, but does not himself believe that which he thinks well of in the case of others. You hear a Jew praising the discipline of the Church, extolling its true grace, honouring the priests of the Church; if you exhort him to believe he refuses, and so follows not himself that which he praises in us. His praise, then, is not full, because Christ said to him: You have rightly judged, for Cain also offered rightly, but did not divide rightly, and therefore God said to him: If you offer rightly, but dividest not rightly, you have sinned, be still. So, then, this man offered rightly, for he judges that Christ ought to be more loved by Christians, because He has forgiven us many sins; but he divided not rightly, because he thought that He could be ignorant of the sins of men Who forgave the sins of men.

11. And, therefore, He said to Simon: You see this woman. I entered into your house, and you gave Me no water for My feet, but she has washed My feet with her tears. Luke 7:44 We are all the one body of Christ, the head of which is God, and we are the members; some perchance eyes, as the prophets; others teeth, as the apostles, who have passed the food of the Gospel preached into our breasts, and rightly is it written: His eyes shall be bright with wine, and his teeth whiter than milk. Genesis 49:12 And His hands are they who are seen to carry out good works, His belly are they who distribute the strength of nourishment on the poor. So, too, some are His feet, and would that I might be worthy to be His heel! He, then, pours water upon the feet of Christ, who forgives the very lowest their offenses, and while delivering those of low estate, yet is washing the feet of Christ.

12. And he pours water upon the feet of Christ, who purifies his conscience from the defilement of sin, for Christ walks in the breast of each. Take heed, then, not to have your conscience polluted, and so to begin to defile the feet of Christ. Take heed lest He encounter a thorn of wickedness in you, whereby as He walks in you His heel may be wounded. For this was why the Pharisee gave no water for the feet of Christ, that he had not a soul pure from the filth of unbelief. For how could he cleanse his conscience who had not received the water of Christ? But the Church both has this water and has tears. For faith which mourns over former sins is wont to guard against fresh ones. Therefore, Simon the Pharisee, who had no water, had also, of course, no tears. For how should he have tears who had no penitence? For since he believed not in Christ he had no tears. For if he had had

them he would have washed his eyes, that he might see Christ, Whom, though he sat at meat with Him, he saw not. For had he seen Him, he would not have doubted of His power.

13. The Pharisee had no hair, inasmuch as he could not recognize the Nazarite; the Church had hair, and she sought the Nazarite. Hairs are counted as among the superfluities of the body, but if they be anointed, they give forth a good odour, and are an ornament to the head; if they be not anointed with oil, are a burden. So, too, riches are a burden if you know not how to use them, and sprinkle them not with the odour of Christ. But if you nourish the poor, if you wash their wounds and wipe away their filth, you have indeed wiped the feet of Christ.

14. You gave Me no kiss, but she from the time she came in has not ceased to kiss My feet. Luke 7:45 A kiss is the sign of love. Whence, then, can a Jew have a kiss, seeing he has not known peace, nor received peace from Christ when He said: My peace I give you, My peace I leave you. John 14:27 The Synagogue has not a kiss, but the Church has, who waited for Him, who loved Him, who said: Let Him kiss me with the kisses of His mouth. Song of Songs 1:2 For by His kisses she wished gradually to quench the burning of that long desire, which had grown with looking for the coming of the Lord, and to satisfy her thirst by this gift. And so the holy prophet says: You shall open my mouth, and it shall declare Your praise. He, then, who praises the Lord Jesus kisses Him, he who praises Him undoubtedly believes. Finally, David himself says: I believed, therefore have I spoken; and before: Let my mouth be filled with Your praise, and let me sing of Your glory.

15. And the same Scripture teaches you concerning the infusion of special grace, that he kisses Christ who receives the Spirit, where the holy prophet says: I opened my mouth and drew in the Spirit. He, then, kisses Christ who confesses Him: For with the heart man believes unto righteousness, and with the mouth confession is made unto salvation. Romans 10:10 He, again, kisses the feet of Christ who, when reading the Gospel, recognizes the acts of the Lord Jesus, and admires them with pious affection, and so piously he kisses, as it were, the footprints of the Lord Jesus as He walks. We kiss Christ, then, with the kiss of communion: Let him that reads understand. Matthew 24:15

16. Whence should the Jew have this kiss? For he who believed in His coming, believed not in His Passion. For how can he believe that He has suffered Whom he believes not to have come? The Pharisee, then, had no kiss except perchance that of the traitor Judas. But neither had Judas the kiss; and so when he wished to show to the Jews that kiss which he had promised as the sign of betrayal, the Lord said to him: Judas, do you betray the Son of Man with a kiss? Luke 22:48 that is, you, who have not the love marked by the kiss, offer a kiss. You offer a kiss who know not the mystery of the kiss. It is not the kiss of the lips which is sought for, but that of the heart and soul.

17. But you say, he kissed the Lord. Yes, he kissed Him indeed with his lips. The Jewish people has this kiss, and therefore it is said: This people honours Me with their lips, but their heart is far from Me. Matthew 15:8 So, then, he who has not faith and charity has not the kiss, for by a kiss the strength of love is impressed.

When love is not, faith is not, and affection is not, what sweetness can there be in kisses?

18. But the Church ceases not to kiss the feet of Christ, and therefore in the Song of Songs she desires not one but many kisses, Song of Songs 1:2 and like Holy Mary she is intent upon all His sayings, and receives all His words when the Gospel or the Prophets are read, and keeps all His sayings in her heart. Luke 2:51 So, then, the Church alone has kisses as a bride, for a kiss is as it were a pledge of espousals and the prerogative of wedlock. Whence should the Jew have kisses, who believes not in the Bridegroom? Whence should the Jew have kisses, who knows not that the Bridegroom has come?

19. And not only has he no kisses, but neither has he oil wherewith to anoint the feet of Christ, for if he had oil he would certainly, before now, soften his own neck.

Moses says: This people is stiff-necked, Exodus 34:9 and the Lord says that the priest and the Levite passed by, and neither of them poured oil or wine into the wounds of him who had been wounded by robbers; Luke 10:31-32 for they had nothing to pour in, since if they had had oil they would have poured it into their own wounds. But Isaiah declares: They cannot apply ointment nor oil nor bandage. Isaiah 1:6

20. But the Church has oil wherewith she dresses the wounds of her children, lest the hardness of the wound spread deeply; she has oil which she has received secretly. With this oil Asher washed his feet as it is written: A blessed son is Asher, and he shall be acceptable to his brothers, and shall dip his feet in oil. Deuteronomy 33:24 With this oil, then, the Church anoints the necks of her children, that they may take up the yoke of Christ; with this oil she anointed the Martyrs, that she might cleanse them from the dust of this world; with this oil she anointed the Confessors, that they might not yield to their labours, nor sink down through weariness; that they might not be overcome by the heat of this world; and she anointed them in order to refresh them with the spiritual oil.

21. The Synagogue has not this oil, inasmuch as she has not the olive, and understood not that dove which brought back the olive branch after the deluge. Genesis 8:11 For that Dove descended afterwards when Christ was baptized, and abode upon Him, as John testified in the Gospel, saying: I saw the Spirit descending from heaven like a dove, and He abode upon Him. John 1:32 But how could he see the Dove, who saw not Him, upon Whom the Spirit descended like a dove?

22. The Church, then, both washes the feet of Christ and wipes them with her hair, and anoints them with oil, and pours ointment upon them, because not only does she care for the wounded and cherish the weary, but also sprinkles them with the sweet odour of grace; and pours forth the same grace not only on the rich and powerful, but also on men of lowly estate. She weighs all with equal balance, gathers all in the same bosom, and cherishes them in the same lap.

23. Christ died once, and was buried once, and nevertheless He wills that ointment should daily be poured on His feet. What, then, are those feet of Christ on which we pour ointment? The feet of Christ are they of whom He Himself says: What you have done to one of the least of these you have done to Me. Matthew 25:40 These feet that woman in the Gospel refreshes, these feet she bedews with her tears; when sin is forgiven to the lowliest, guilt is washed away, and pardon granted. These feet he kisses, who loves even the lowest of the holy people. These feet he anoints with ointment, who imparts the kindness of his gentleness even to the weaker. In these the martyrs, in these the apostles, in these the Lord Jesus Himself declares that He is honoured.

24. You see how ready to teach the Lord is, that He may by His own example provoke you to piety, for He is ready to teach when He rebukes. So when accusing the Jews, He says: O My people, what have I done to you, or wherein have I troubled you, or wherein have I wearied you? Answer Me. Is it because I brought you out of the land of Egypt, and delivered you from the house of bondage? adding: And I sent before your face Moses and Aaron and Miriam. Remember what Balaam conceived against you, Numbers 23:2 seeking the aid of magic art, but I suffered him not to hurt you. You were indeed weighed down an exile in foreign lands, you were oppressed with heavy burdens. I sent before your face Moses and Aaron and Miriam, and he who spoiled the exile was first spoiled himself. You who had lost what was yours, obtained that which was another's, being freed from the enemies who were hedging you in, and safe in the midst of the waters you saw the destruction of your enemies, when the same waves which surrounded and carried you on your way, pouring back, drowned the enemy. Exodus 14:29 Did I not, when food was lacking to you passing through the desert, supply a rain of food, and nourishment around you, wherever you went? Did I not, after subduing all your enemies, bring you into the region of Eshcol? Numbers 13:24 Did I not deliver up you Sihon, King of the Amorites Numbers 21:24 (that is, the proud one, the leader of them that provoked you)? Did I not deliver up to you alive the King of Ai, whom after the ancient curse you condemned to be fastened to the wood and raised upon the cross? Why should I speak of the troops of the five kings which were slain in endeavouring to deny you the land given to you? And now what is required of you in return for all this, but to do judgment and justice, to love mercy, and to be ready to walk with the Lord your God? Micah 6:8

25. And what was His expostulation by Nathan the prophet to King David himself, that pious and gentle man? I, He said, chose you the youngest of your brethren, I filled you with the spirit of meekness, I anointed you king by the hand of Samuel, in whom I and My Name dwelt. Having removed that former king, whom an evil spirit stirred up to persecute the priests of the Lord, I made you triumph after exile. I set upon your throne of your seed one not more an heir than a colleague. I made even strangers subject to you, that they who attacked might serve you, and will you deliver My servants into the power of My enemies, and will you take away that which was My servant's, whereby both yourself will be branded with sin, and My adversaries will have whereof to rejoice.

26. Wherefore, O Emperor, that I may now address my words not only about you, but to you, since you observe how severely the Lord is wont to censure, see that the more glorious you have become, the more utterly you submit to your Maker. For it is written: When the Lord your God shall have brought you into a strange land, and you shall eat the fruits of others, say not, My power and my righteousness has given me this, for the Lord your God has given it to you; for Christ in His mercy has conferred it on you, and therefore, in love for His body, that is, the Church, give water for His feet, kiss His feet, so that you may not only pardon those who have been taken in sin, but also by your peaceableness restore them to concord, and give them rest. Pour ointment upon His feet that the whole house in which Christ sits may be filled with your ointment, and all that sit with Him may rejoice in your fragrance, that is, honour the lowest, so that the angels may rejoice in their forgiveness, as over one sinner that repents, Luke 15:10 the apostles may be glad, the prophets be filled with delight. For the eyes cannot say to the hand: We have no need of you, nor the head to the feet, You are not necessary to me. 1 Corinthians 12:21 So, since all are necessary, guard the whole body of the Lord Jesus, that He also by His heavenly condescension may preserve your kingdom.

27. When I came down from the pulpit, he said to me: You spoke about me. I replied: I dealt with matters intended for your benefit. Then he said: I had indeed decided too harshly about the repairing of the synagogue by the bishop, but that has been rectified. The monks commit many crimes. Then Timasius the general began to be over-vehement against the monks, and I answered him: With the Emperor I deal as is fitting, because I know that he has the fear of God, but with you, who speak so roughly, one must deal otherwise.

28. Then, after standing for some time, I said to the Emperor: Let me offer for you without anxiety, set my mind at ease. As he continued sitting and nodded, but did not give an open promise, and I remained standing, he said that he would amend the edict. I went on at once to say that he must end the whole investigation, lest the Count should use the opportunity of the investigation to do any injury to the Christians. He promised that it should be so. I said to him, I act on your promise, and repeated, I act on your promise. Act, he said, on my promise. And so I went to the altar, whither I should not have gone unless he had given me a distinct promise. And indeed so great was the grace attending the offering, that I felt myself that that favour granted by the Emperor was very acceptable to our God, and that the divine presence was not wanting. And so everything was done as I wished.

LETTER LI

Addressed to the Emperor Theodosius after the massacre at Thessalonica. St. Ambrose begins by stating his reasons for not having met the Emperor on his return to Milan. He then mentions the sentiments of the bishops with regard to the slaughter at Thessalonica, and points out that repentance for that deed is necessary to obtain forgiveness and a victory over the devil, the instigator to that crime. St. Ambrose could not offer the sacrifice in the Emperor's presence, and, as truly loving the Emperor, grieves and yet hopes.

1. The memory of your old friendship is pleasant to me, and I gratefully call to mind the kindnesses which, in reply to my frequent intercessions, you have most graciously conferred on others. Whence it may be inferred that I did not from any ungrateful feeling avoid meeting you on your arrival, which I had always before earnestly desired. And I will now briefly set forth the reason for my acting as I did.

2. I saw that from me alone in your court the natural right of hearing was withdrawn, so that I was deprived also of the office of speaking; for you were frequently troubled because certain matters which had been decided in your consistory had come to my knowledge. I, therefore, am without a part in the common privilege, since the Lord Jesus says: That nothing is hidden, which shall not be made known. Luke 8:17 I, therefore, as reverently as I could, complied with the imperial will, and took heed that neither yourself should have any reason for displeasure, when I effected that nothing should be related to me of the imperial decrees; and that I, when present, either should not hear, through fear of all others, and so incur the reputation of connivance, or should hear in such a fashion that my ears might be open, my utterance prevented, that I might not be able to utter what I had heard lest I should injure and bring in peril those who had incurred the suspicion of treachery.

3. What, then, could I do? Should I not hear? But I could not close my ears with the wax of the old fables. Should I utter what I heard? But I was bound to be on my guard in my words against that which I feared in your commands, namely, lest some deed of blood should be committed. Should I keep silence? But then my conscience would be bound, my utterance taken away, which would be the most wretched condition of all. And where would be that text? If the priest speak not to him that errs, he who errs shall die in his sin, and the priest shall be liable to the penalty because he warned not the erring. Ezekiel 3:18

4. Listen, august Emperor. I cannot deny that you have a zeal for the faith; I do confess that you have the fear of God. But you have a natural vehemence, which, if any one endeavours to soothe, you quickly turn to mercy; if any one stirs it up, you rouse it so much more that you can scarcely restrain it. Would that if no one soothe it, at least no one may inflame it! To yourself I willingly entrust it, you restrain yourself, and overcome your natural vehemence by the love of piety.

5. This vehemence of yours I preferred to commend privately to your own consideration, rather than possibly raise it by any action of mine in public. And so I have preferred to be somewhat wanting in duty rather than in humility, and that other, should rather think me wanting in priestly authority than that you should find me lacking in most loving reverence, that having restrained your vehemence

your power of deciding on your counsel should not be weakened. I excuse myself by bodily sickness, which was in truth severe, and scarcely to be lightened but by great care. Yet I would rather have died than not wait two or three days for your arrival. But it was not possible for me to do so.

6. There was that done in the city of the Thessalonians of which no similar record exists, which I was not able to prevent happening; which, indeed, I had before said would be most atrocious when I so often petitioned against it, and that which you yourself show by revoking it too late you consider to be grave, this I could not extenuate when done. When it was first heard of, a synod had met because of the arrival of the Gallican Bishops. There was not one who did not lament it, not one who thought lightly of it; your being in fellowship with Ambrose was no excuse for your deed. Blame for what had been done would have been heaped more and more on me, had no one said that your reconciliation to our God was necessary.

7. Are you ashamed, O Emperor, to do that which the royal prophet David, the forefather of Christ, according to the flesh, did? To him it was told how the rich man who had many flocks seized and killed the poor man's one lamb, because of the arrival of his , and recognizing that he himself was being condemned in the tale, for that he himself had done it, he said: I have sinned against the Lord. Bear it, then, without impatience, O Emperor, if it be said to you: You have done that which was spoken of to King David by the prophet. For if you listen obediently to this, and say: I have sinned against the Lord, if you repeat those words of the royal prophet: O come let us worship and fall down before Him, and mourn before the Lord our God, Who made us, it shall be said to you also: Since you repent, the Lord puts away your sin, and you shall not die.

8. And again, David, after he had commanded the people to be numbered, was smitten in heart, and said to the Lord: I have sinned exceedingly, because I have commanded this, and now, O Lord, take away the iniquity of Your servant, for I have transgressed exceedingly. And the prophet Nathan was sent again to him, to offer him the choice of three things, that he should select the one he chose — famine in the land for three years, or that he should flee for three months before his enemies, or mortal pestilence in the land for three days. And David answered: These three things are a great strait to me, but let me fall into the hand of the Lord, for very many are His mercies, and let me not fall into the hands of man. Now his fault was that he desired to know the number of the whole of the people which was with him, which knowledge he ought to have left to God alone.

9. And, we are told, when death came upon the people, on the very first day at dinner time, when David saw the angel smiting the people, he said: I have sinned, and I, the shepherd, have done wickedly, and this flock, what has it done? Let Your hand be upon me, and upon my father's house. And so it repented the Lord, and He commanded the angel to spare the people, and David to offer a sacrifice, for sacrifices were then offered for sins; sacrifices are now those of penitence. And so by that humbling of himself he became more acceptable to God, for it is no matter of wonder that a man should sin, but this is reprehensible, if he does not recognize that he has erred, and humble himself before God.

10. Holy Job, himself also powerful in this world, says: I hid not my sin, but declared it before all the people. His son Jonathan said to the fierce King Saul himself: Do not sin against your servant David; and: Why do you sin against innocent blood, to slay David without a cause? For, although he was a king, yet he would have sinned if he slew the innocent. And again, David also, when he was in possession of the kingdom, and had heard that innocent Abner had been slain by Joab, the leader of his host, said: I am guiltless and my kingdom is guiltless henceforth and for ever of the blood of Abner, the son of Ner, and he fasted for sorrow.

11. I have written this, not in order to confound you, but that the examples of these kings may stir you up to put away this sin from your kingdom, for you will do it away by humbling your soul before God. You are a man, and it has come upon you, conquer it. Sin is not done away but by tears and penitence. Neither angel can do it, nor archangel. The Lord Himself, Who alone can say, I am with you, Matthew 28:20 if we have sinned, does not forgive any but those who repent.

12. I urge, I beg, I exhort, I warn, for it is a grief to me, that you who were an example of unusual piety, who were conspicuous for clemency, who would not suffer single offenders to be put in peril, should not mourn that so many have perished. Though you have waged battle most successfully, though in other matters, too, you are worthy of praise, yet piety was ever the crown of your actions. The devil envied that which was your most excellent possession. Conquer him while you still possess that wherewith you may conquer. Do not add another sin to your sin by a course of action which has injured many.

13. I, indeed, though a debtor to your kindness, for which I cannot be ungrateful, that kindness which has surpassed that of many emperors, and has been equalled by one only; I, I say, have no cause for a charge of contumacy against you, but have cause for fear; I dare not offer the sacrifice if you intend to be present. Is that which is not allowed after shedding the blood of one innocent person, allowed after shedding the blood of many? I do not think so.

14. Lastly, I am writing with my own hand that which you alone may read. As I hope that the Lord will deliver me from all troubles, I have been warned, not by man, nor through man, but plainly by Himself that this is forbidden me. For when I was anxious, in the very night in which I was preparing to set out, you appeared to me in a dream to have come into the Church, and I was not permitted to offer the sacrifice. I pass over other things, which I could have avoided, but I bore them for love of you, as I believe. May the Lord cause all things to pass peaceably. Our God gives warnings in many ways, by heavenly signs, by the precepts of the prophets; by the visions even of sinners He wills that we should understand, that we should entreat Him to take away all disturbances, to preserve peace for you emperors, that the faith and peace of the Church, whose advantage it is that emperors should be Christians and devout, may continue.

15. You certainly desire to be approved by God. To everything there is a time, Ecclesiastes 3:1 as it is written: It is time for You, Lord, to work. It is an acceptable time, O Lord. You shall then make your offering when you have

received permission to sacrifice, when your offering shall be acceptable to God. Would it not delight me to enjoy the favour of the Emperor, to act according to your wish, if the case allowed it? And prayer by itself is a sacrifice, it obtains pardon, when the oblation would bring offense, for the one is a sign of humility, the other of contempt. For the Word of God Himself tells us that He prefers the performance of His commandments to the offering of sacrifice. God proclaims this, Moses declares it to the people, Paul preaches it to the Gentiles. Do that which you understand is most profitable for the time. I prefer mercy, it is said, rather than sacrifice. Matthew 9:13 Are they not, then, rather Christians in truth who condemn their own sin, than they who think to defend it? The just is an accuser of himself in the beginning of his words. He who accuses himself when he has sinned is just, not he who praises himself.

16. I wish, O Emperor, that before this I had trusted rather to myself, than to your habits. When I consider that you quickly pardon, and quickly revoke your sentence, as you have often done; you have been anticipated, and I have not shunned that which I needed not to fear. But thanks be to the Lord, Who wills to chastise His servants, that He may not lose them. This I have in common with the prophets, and you shall have it in common with the saints.

17. Shall I not value the father of Gratian more than my very eyes? Your other holy pledges also claim pardon. I conferred beforehand a dear name on those to whom I bore a common love. I follow you with my love, my affection, and my prayers. If you believe me, be guided by me; if, I say, you believe me, acknowledge what I say; if you believe me not, pardon that which I do, in that I set God before you. May you, most august Emperor, with your holy offspring, enjoy perpetual peace with perfect happiness and prosperity.

LETTER LVII

St. Ambrose informs the Emperor Eugenius why he was absent from Milan. He then proceeds to reprove him for his conduct with regard to heathen worship. This was, he says, the reason why he did not write sooner, and he promises that for the future he will treat him with the same freedom as the other emperors.

Ambrose, Bishop, to the most gracious Emperor Eugenius.

1. The cause of my departure was the fear of the Lord, to Whom, so far as I am able, I am accustomed to refer all my acts, and never to turn away my mind from Him, nor to make more of any man than of the grace of Christ. For I do no one an injury, if I set God before all, and, trusting in Him, I am not afraid to tell you emperors my thoughts, such as they are. And so I will not keep silence before you, O Emperor, as to things respecting which I have not kept silence before other emperors. And that I may keep the order of the matters, I will go through, one by one, the things which have to do with this matter.

2. The illustrious Symmachus, when prefect of the city, had memorialized the Emperor Valentinian the younger of august memory, requesting that he would command that what had been taken away should be restored to the temples. He performed his part in accordance with his zeal and his religion. And I also, as Bishop, was bound to recognize my part. I presented two petitions to the Emperors, in which I pointed out that a Christian man could not contribute to the cost of the sacrifices; that I indeed had not been the cause of their being abolished, but I certainly did urge that they should not be decreed; and lastly, that he himself would seem to be giving not restoring those sums to the images. For what he had not himself taken away, he could not, as it were, restore, but of his own will to grant towards the expenses of superstition. Lastly, that, if he did it, either he must not come to the Church, or, if he came, he would either not find a priest there, or he would find one withstanding him in the Church. Nor could it be alleged in excuse that he was a catechumen, seeing that catechumens are not allowed to contribute to the idols' expenses.

3. My letters were read in the consistory. Count Bauto, a man of the highest rank of military authority was present, and Rumoridus, himself also of the same dignity, addicted to the worship of the gentile nations from the first years of his boyhood. Valentinian at that time listened to my suggestion, and did nothing but what the rule of our faith required. And they yielded to his officer.

4. Afterwards I plainly addressed the most clement Emperor Theodosius, and hesitated not to speak to his face. And he, having received a similar message from the Senate, though it was not the request of the whole Senate, at length assented to my recommendation, and so I did not go near him for some days, nor did he take it ill, for he knew that I was not acting for my own advantage, but was not ashamed to say in the sight of the king that which was for the profit of himself and of my own soul.

5. Again a legation sent into Gaul from the Senate to the Emperor Valentinian of august memory could procure nothing; and then I was certainly absent, and had not written anything at that time to him.

6. But when your Clemency took up the reins of government it was afterwards discovered that favours of this kind had been granted to men, excellent indeed in matters of state but in religion heathens. And it may, perhaps, be said, august Emperor, that you did not make any restitution to temples, but presented gifts to men who had deserved well of you. But you know that we must constantly act in the cause of God, as is often done in the cause of liberty, also not only by priests, but also by those who are in your armies, or are reckoned in the number of those who dwell in the provinces. When you became Emperor envoys requested that you would make restitution to the temples, and you did not do it; others came a second time and you resisted, and afterwards you thought fit that this should be granted to those very persons who made the petition.

7. Though the imperial power be great, yet consider, O Emperor, how great God is. He sees the hearts of all, He questions the inmost conscience, He knows all things before they happen, He knows the inmost things of your breast. You do not suffer yourselves to be deceived, and do you desire to conceal anything from God? Has not this come into your mind? For although they acted with such perseverance, was it not your duty, O Emperor, to resist with still greater perseverance because of the reverence due to the most high and true and living God, and to refuse what was an offense against His holy law?

8. Who grudges your having given what you would to others? We are not scrutinizers of your liberality, nor envious of the advantages of others, but are interpreters of the faith. How will you offer your gifts to Christ? Not many but will put their own estimate on what you have done, all will do so on your intentions. Whatever they do will be ascribed to you; whatever they do not do, to themselves. Although you are Emperor, you ought to be all the more subject to God. How shall the ministers of Christ dispense your gifts?

9. There was a question of this sort in former times, and yet persecution itself yielded to the faith of our fathers, and heathendom gave way. For when in the city of Tyre the quinquennial game was being kept, and the intensely wicked King of Antioch had come to witness it, Jason appointed officers of sacred rites, who were Antiochians, to carry three hundred didrachms of silver from Jerusalem, and give them to the sacrifice of Hercules. But the fathers did not give the money to the heathen, but having sent faithful men declared that that money should not be spent on sacrifices to the gods, because it was not fitting, but on other expenses. And it was decreed that because he had said that the money was sent for the sacrifice of Hercules, it ought to be taken for that for which it was sent; but, because they, who had brought it, because of their zeal and religion, pleaded that it should not be used for the sacrifice, but for other expenses, the money was given for the building of ships. Being compelled they sent it, but it was not used for sacrifice, but for other expenses of the state.

10. Now they who had brought the money might, no doubt, have kept silence, but would have done violence to their faith, because they knew whither the money was being carried, and therefore they sent men who feared God to contrive that what was sent should be assigned, not to the temple, but to the cost of ships. For they entrusted the money to those who should plead the cause of the sacred Law, and He Who absolves the conscience was made judge of the matter. If they when in the power of another were so careful, there can be no doubt what you, O Emperor, ought to have done. You, at any rate, whom no one compelled, whom no one had in his power, ought to have sought counsel from the priest.

11. And I certainly when I then resisted, although I was alone in resistance, was not alone in what I wished, and was not alone in what I advised. Since, then, I am bound by my own words both before God and before all men, I felt that nothing else was allowable or needful for me but to act for myself, because I could not well trust you. I kept back and concealed my grief for a long time; I thought it not right to intimate anything to anybody, now I may no longer dissemble, nor is it open to me to keep silence. For this reason also at the commencement of your reign I did not reply when you wrote to me, because I foresaw that this would happen. Then at last, when you required a letter, because I had not written a reply, I said: This is the reason that I think this will be extorted from him.

12. But when a reason for exercising my office arose, I both wrote and petitioned for those who were in anxiety about themselves, that I might show that in the canse of God I felt a righteous fear, and that I did not value flattery above my own soul; but in those matters in which it is fitting that petitions should be addressed to you. I also pay the deference due to authority, as it is written: Honour to whom honour is due, tribute to whom tribute. Romans 13:7 For since I deferred from the bottom of my heart to a private person, how could I not defer to the Emperor? But do you who desire that deference be paid to you suffer us to pay deference to Him Whom you are desirous to be proved the Author of your power.

LETTER LXI

St. Ambrose explains his absence from Milan on the arrival of the Emperor Theodosius after his victory over Eugenius, and after expressing his thankfulness for that success he promises obedience to the Emperor's will, and while commending his piety urges him to be merciful to the conquered.

Ambrose, to the Emperor Theodosius.

1. You thought, most blessed Emperor, so far as I gathered from your letter, that I kept away from the city of Milan, because I believed that your cause was forsaken by God. But I was not so wanting in foresight, nor so unmindful in my absence of your virtue and merits, as not to anticipate that the aid of Heaven would be with your piety, with which you would rescue the Roman Empire from the cruelty of a barbarian robber, and the dominion of an unworthy usurper.

2. I therefore made haste to return there, as soon as I knew that he, whom I thought it right to avoid, was now gone, for I had not deserted the Church of Milan, entrusted to me by the judgment of God, but avoided the presence of him who had involved himself in sacrilege. I returned, therefore, about the Calends of August, and have resided here since that day. Here, too, O Augustus, your letter found me.

3. Thanks be to our Lord God, Who responded to your faith and piety, and has restored the form of ancient sanctity, suffering us to see in our time that which we wonder at in reading the Scriptures, namely, such a presence of the divine assistance in battle, that no mountain heights delayed the course of your approach, no hostile arms were any hindrance.

4. For these mercies you think that I ought to render thanks to the Lord our God, and being conscious of your merits, I will do so willingly. Certainly that offering will be acceptable to God which is offered in your name, and what a mark of faith and devotion is this! Other emperors, immediately upon a victory, order the erection of triumphal arches, or other monuments of their triumphs; your Clemency prepares an offering for God, and desires that oblation and thanksgiving should be presented by the priests to the Lord.

5. Though I be unworthy and unequal to such an office and the offering of such acknowledgments, yet will I describe what I have done. I took the letter of your Piety with me to the altar. I laid it upon the altar. I held it in my hand while I offered the Sacrifice; so that your faith might speak by my voice, and the Emperor's letter discharge the function of the priestly oblation.

6. In truth, the Lord is propitious to the Roman Empire, since He has chosen such a prince and father of princes, whose virtue and power, established on such a triumphant height of dominion, rests on such humility, that in valour he has surpassed emperors and priests in humility. What can I wish? What can I desire? You have everything, and therefore I will endeavour to gain the sum of my desires. You, O Emperor, are pitiful, and of the greatest clemency.

7. And for yourself, I desire again and again an increase of piety, than which God has given nothing more excellent, that by your clemency the Church of God, as it delights in the peace and tranquillity of the innocent, so, too, may rejoice in the pardon of the guilty. Pardon especially those who have not offended before. May the Lord preserve your Clemency. Amen.

LETTER LXII

St. Ambrose excuses himself for having omitted an opportunity of writing to the Emperor, but is now sending a letter by the hands of a deacon, requesting forgiveness for some of Eugenius' followers who had sought the protection of the Church, especially in consideration of the miraculous aid which had been vouchsafed to the Emperor.

Ambrose, to the Emperor Theodosius.

1. Although I lately wrote to your Clemency even a second time, it did not seem to me that I had responded sufficiently to the duty of intercourse by answering as it were in turn, for I have been so bound by frequent benefits from your Clemency, that I cannot repay what I owe by any services, most blessed and august Emperor.

2. And so just as the first opportunity was not to be lost by me, when, through your chamberlain, I was able to thank your Clemency and to pay the duty of an address, especially lest my not having written before should seem to have been owing to sloth rather than necessity, so, too, I had to seek some manner of rendering to your Piety my dutiful salutations.

3. And rightly do I send my son, the deacon Felix, to bear my letter, and, at the same time, to present to you my duty, in my place, and also a memorial on behalf of those who have fled to the Church, the Mother of your Piety, seeking mercy. I have been unable to endure their tears without anticipating by my entreaty the coming of your Clemency.

4. It is a great boon that I ask, but I ask it from him to whom the Lord has granted great and unheard-of things, from him whose clemency I know, and whose piety I have as a pledge. For your victory is considered to have been granted to you after the ancient manner, and with the old miracles, a victory such as was granted to holy Moses, and holy Joshua, son of Nave, and Samuel, and David, not by human calculations, but by the outpouring of heavenly grace. Now we expect an equal amount of gentleness with that by virtue of which so great a victory has been gained.

LETTER LXIII

Limenius, Bishop of Vercellæ, having died, the see remained long vacant owing to domestic factions. St. Ambrose, therefore, as Exarch, writes to the Christians at Vercellæ, and commences by reference to the speedy and unanimous election of Eusebius, a former Bishop, and reminds them of the presence of Christ as a reason for concord. He refers next to two apostate monks, Sarmatio and Barbatianus, and inveighs against sensuality, which degrades men below the beasts. Thence he passes to the virtues required in a bishop, referring again to Eusebius, and to Dionysius, Bishop of Milan, comparing the clerical and monastic lives, and ends with exhortations to Christian virtue. The letter seems to have been written a.d. 396.

Ambrose, a servant of Christ, called to be a Bishop, to the Church of Vercellæ, and to those who call on the Name of our Lord Jesus Christ, Grace be fulfilled unto you in the Holy Spirit from God the Father and His only-begotten Son.

1. I am spent with grief that the Church of God which is among you is still without a bishop, and now alone of all the regions of Liguria and Æmilia, and of the Venetiæ and other neighbouring parts of Italy needs that care which other churches were wont to ask for themselves from it; and what is a greater source of shame to myself, the tension among you which causes the obstacle is laid to my charge. Now since there are dissensions among you, how can we decree anything, or you elect, or anyone agree to undertake this office among those who are at variance which he could hardly sustain among those who are at unity.

2. Is this the training of a confessor, are these the offspring of those righteous fathers who, as soon as they saw, approved of holy Eusebius, whom they had never known before, preferring him to their fellow citizens, and he was no sooner among them than he was approved, and much more when they had observed him. Justly did he turn out so great a man, whom the whole Church elected, justly was it believed that he whom all had demanded was elected by the judgment of God. It is fitting then that you follow the example of your parents, especially since you who have been instructed by a holy confessor ought to be so much better than your fathers, as a better teacher has taught and instructed you, and to manifest a sign of your moderation and concord by agreeing in your request for a Bishop.

3. For if according to the Lord's saying, that which two shall have agreed upon on earth concerning anything which they shall ask, shall be done for them, as He says, by My Father, Who is in heaven, for: Where two or three are gathered together in My Name, there am I in the midst of them, Matthew 18:21 how much less, where the full congregation is gathered in the Name of the Lord. Where the demand of all is unanimous, ought we to doubt that the Lord Jesus is there as the Author of that desire, and the Hearer of the petition, the Presider over the ordination, and the Giver of the grace?

4. Make yourselves then to appear worthy that Christ should be in your midst. For where peace is, there is Christ, for Christ is Peace; and where righteousness is, there is Christ, for Christ is Righteousness. Let Him be in the midst of you, that you may see Him, lest it be said to you also: There stands One in the midst of you, Whom you see not. John 1:26 The Jews saw not Him in Whom they believed not; we look upon Him by devotion, and behold Him by faith.

5. Let Him therefore stand in your midst, that the heavens, which declare the glory of God, may be opened to you, that you may do His will, and work His works. He who sees Jesus, to him are the heavens opened as they were opened to Stephen, when he said: Behold I see the heavens opened and Jesus standing at the right hand of God. Acts 7:56 Jesus was standing as his advocate, He was standing as though anxious, that He might help His athlete Stephen in his conflict, He was standing as though ready to crown His martyr.

6. Let Him then be standing for you, that you may not be afraid of Him sitting; for when sitting He judges, as Daniel says: The thrones were placed, and the books were opened, and the Ancient of days did sit. Daniel 7:9 But in the eighty-first [second] Psalm it is written: God stood in the congregation of gods, and decides among the gods. So then when He sits He judges, when He stands He decides, and He judges concerning the imperfect, but decides among the gods. Let Him stand for you as a defender, as a good shepherd, lest the fierce wolves assault you.

7. And not in vain is my warning turned to this point; for I hear that Sarmatio and Barbatianus have come to you, foolish talkers, who say that there is no merit in abstinence, no grace in a frugal life, none in virginity, that all are valued at one price, that they are mad who chasten their flesh with fastings, that they may bring it into subjection to the spirit. But if he had thought it madness, Paul the Apostle would never himself have acted thus, nor written to instruct others. For he glories in it, saying: But I chasten my body, and bring it into bondage, lest, after preaching to others, I myself should be found reprobate. 1 Corinthians 9:27 So they who do not chasten their body, and desire to preach to others, are themselves esteemed reprobates.

8. For is there anything so reprobate as that which excites to luxury, to corruption, to wantonness, as the incentive to lust, the enticer to pleasure, the fuel of incontinence, the firebrand of desire? What new school has sent out these Epicureans? Not a school of philosophers, as they themselves say, but of unlearned men who preach pleasure, persuade to luxury, esteem chastity to be of no use. They were with us, but they were not of us, John 2:19 for we are not ashamed to say what the Evangelist John said. But when settled here they used to fast at first, they were enclosed within the monastery, there was no place for luxury, the opportunity of mocking and disputing was cut off.

9. This these dainty men could not endure. They went abroad, then when they desired to return they were not received; for I had heard many things which necessitated my being cautious; I admonished them, but effected nothing. And so boiling over they began to disseminate such things as made them the miserable enticers to all vices. They utterly lost the benefit of having fasted; they lost the fruits of their temporary continence. And so now they with Satanic eagerness envy the good works of others, the fruit of which themselves have failed to keep.

10. What virgin can hear that there is no reward for her chastity and not groan? Far be it from her to believe this easily, and still more to lay aside her zeal, or change the intention of her mind. What widow, when she learned that there was no profit in her widowhood, would choose to preserve her marriage faith and live in sorrow,

rather than give herself up to a happier condition? Who, bound by the marriage-bond, if she hear that there is no honour in chastity, might not be tempted by careless levity of body or mind? And for this reason the Church in the holy lessons, and in the addresses of her priests, proclaims the praise of chastity and the glory of virginity.

11. In vain, then, does the Apostle say: I wrote to you, in an Epistle, not to mingle with fornicators; 1 Corinthians 5:9 and lest perchance they should say, We are not speaking of all the fornicators of the world, but we say that he who has been baptized in Christ ought not now to be esteemed a fornicator, but his life, whatever it is, is accepted of God, the Apostle has added Not at all [meaning] with the fornicators of this world, and farther on, If any that is named a brother be a fornicator, or covetous, or an idolator, or a reviler, or a drunkard, or an extortioner, with such an one not even to eat. For what have I to do with judging them that are without? 1 Corinthians 5:10-11 And to the Ephesians: But fornication, and all uncleanness, and covetousness let it not even be named among you, as becomes saints. Ephesians 5:3 And immediately he adds: For this you know, that no immodest person, nor unclean, nor covetous, which is an idolator, has any inheritance in the kingdom of Christ and of God. Ephesians 5:5 It is clear that this is said of the baptized, for they receive the inheritance, who are baptized into the death of Christ Romans 6:3 and are buried together with Him, that they may rise again with Him. Therefore they are heirs of God, and joint heirs with Christ: Romans 8:17 heirs of God, because the grace of Christ is conveyed to them; joint-heirs with Christ, because they are renewed into His life; heirs also of Christ; because to them is given by His death as it were the inheritance of the testator.

12. These then ought to take heed to themselves who have that which they may lose, rather than they who have it not. These ought to act with greater care, these ought to guard against the allurements of vice, or incentives to error, which arise chiefly from food and drink. For the people sat down to eat and drink, and rose up to play. 1 Corinthians 10:7

13. Epicurus himself also, whom these persons think they should follow rather than the apostles, the advocate of pleasure, although he denies that pleasure brings in evil, does not deny that certain things result from it from which evils are generated; and asserts in fine that the life of the luxurious which is filled with pleasures does not seem to be reprehensible, unless it be disturbed by the fear either of pain or of death. But how far he is from the truth is perceived even from this, that he asserts that pleasure was originally created in man by God its author, as Philomarus his follower argues in his Epitomæ, asserting that the Stoics are the authors of this opinion.

14. But Holy Scripture refutes this, for it teaches us that pleasure was suggested to Adam and Eve by the craft and enticements of the serpent. Since, indeed, the serpent itself is pleasure, and therefore the passions of pleasure are various and slippery, and as it were infected with the poison of corruptions, it is certain then that Adam, being deceived by the desire of pleasure, fell away from the commandment of God and from the enjoyment of grace. How then can pleasure recall us to paradise, seeing that it alone deprived us of it?

15. Wherefore also the Lord Jesus, wishing to make us more strong against the temptations of the devil, fasted when about to contend with him, that we might know that we can in no other way overcome the enticements of evil. Further, the devil himself hurled the first dart of his temptations from the quiver of pleasure, saying: If You be the Son of God, command that these stones become bread. Matthew 4:3 After which the Lord said: Man does not live by bread alone, but by every word of God; Matthew 4:4 and would not do it, although He could, in order to teach us by a salutary precept to attend rather to the pursuit of reading than to pleasure. And since they say that we ought not to fast, let them prove for what cause Christ fasted, unless it were that His fast might be an example to us. Lastly, in His later words He taught us that evil cannot be easily overcome except by our fasting, saying: This kind of devils is not cast out but by prayer and fasting. Matthew 17:21

16. And what is the intention of the Scripture which teaches us that Peter fasted, and that the revelation concerning the baptism of Gentiles was made to him when fasting and praying, Acts 10:10 except to show that the Saints themselves advance when they fast. Finally, Moses received the Law when he was fasting; Exodus 34:28 and so Peter when fasting was taught the grace of the New Testament. Daniel too by virtue of his fast stopped the mouths of the lions and saw the events of future times. Daniel vi.-vii And what safety can there be for us unless we wash away our sins by fasting, since Scripture says that fasting and alms do away sin? Tobit 12:8-9

17. Who then are these new teachers who reject the merit of fasting? Is it not the voice of heathen who say, Let us eat and drink? whom the Apostle well ridicules, when he says: If after the manner of men I have fought with beasts at Ephesus, what advantages it me if the dead rise not? Let us eat and drink, for tomorrow we die. 1 Corinthians 15:32 That is to say, What profited me my contention even unto death, except that I might redeem my body? And it is redeemed in vain if there is no hope of the resurrection. And, consequently, if all hope of the resurrection is lost, let us eat and drink, let us not lose the enjoyment of things present, who have none of things to come. It is then for them to indulge in meats and drinks who hope for nothing after death.

18. Rightly then does the Apostle, arguing against these men, warn us that we be not shaken by such opinions, saying: Be not deceived, evil communications corrupt good manners. Be righteously sober and sin not, for some have no knowledge of God. 1 Corinthians 15:33 Sobriety, then, is good, for drunkenness is sin.

19. But as to that Epicurus himself, the defender of pleasure, of whom, therefore, we have made frequent mention in order to prove that these men are either disciples of the heathen and followers of the Epicurean sect or himself, whom the very philosophers exclude from their company as the patron of luxury, what if we prove him to be more tolerable than these men? He declares, as Demarchus asserts, that neither drinking, nor banquets, nor offspring, nor embraces of women, nor abundance of fish, and other such like things which are prepared for the service of a sumptuous banquet, make life sweet, but sober discussion. Lastly, he

added that those who do not use the banquets of society in excess, use them with moderation. He who willingly makes use of the juices of plants alone together with bread and water, despises feasts on delicacies, for many inconveniences arise from them. In another place they also say: It is not excessive banquets, nor drinking which give rise to the enjoyment of pleasure, but a life of temperance.

20. Since, then, philosophy has disowned those men, is the Church not to exclude them? Seeing, too, that they, because they have a bad cause, frequently fall foul of themselves by their own assertions. For, although their chief opinion is that there is no enjoyment of pleasure except such as is derived from eating and drinking, yet understanding that they cannot, without the greatest shame, cling to so disgraceful a definition, and that they are forsaken by all, they have tried to color it with a sort of stain of specious arguments; so that one of them has said: Whilst we are aiming at pleasure by means of banquets and songs, we have lost that which is infused into us by the reception of the Word, whereby alone we can be saved.

21. Do not they by these various arguments show themselves to us as differing and disagreeing one with the other? And Scripture too condemns them, not passing over those whom the Apostle refuted, as Luke, who wrote the book as a history, tells us in the Acts of the Apostles, And certain also of the Epicurean and Stoic philosophers disputed with him. And some said, What does this babbler mean? And others said, He seems to be a setter forth of new gods. Acts 17:18

22. Yet from this hand too the Apostle did not go forth without success, since even Dionysius the Areopagite together with his wife Damaris and many others believed. And so that company of most learned and eloquent men showed themselves overcome in a simple discussion by the example of those who believed. What then do those men mean, who endeavour to prevent those whom the Apostle has gained, and whom Christ has redeemed with His own blood? Asserting that the baptized ought not to give themselves to the discipline of the virtues, that revellings injure them not, nor abundance of pleasures; that they are foolish who go without them, that virgins ought to marry, bear children, and likewise widows to repeat that converse with man which they have once experienced with ill results; and that even if they can contain, they are in error who will not again enter the marriage bond.

23. What then? Would you have us put off the man in order to put on the beast, and stripping ourselves of Christ, clothe ourselves or be superclothed with the garments of the devil? But since the very teachers of the heathen did not think that honour and pleasure could be joined together, because they would seem thus to class beasts with men, shall we as it were infuse the habits of beasts into the human breast, and inscribe on the reasonable mind the unreasoning ways of wild beasts?

24. And yet there are many kinds of animals, which, when they have lost their fellow, will not mate again, and spend their time as it were in solitary life; many too live on simple herbs, and will not quench their thirst except at a pure stream; one can also often see dogs refrain from food forbidden them, so that they close

their famishing mouths if restraint is bidden them. Must men then be warned against that wherein brutes have learned not to transgress?

26. But what is more admirable than abstinence, which makes even the years of youth to ripen, so that there is an old age of character? For as by excess of food and by drunkenness even mature age is excited, so the wildness of youth is lessened by scanty feasts and by the running stream. An external fire is extinguished by pouring on water, it is then no wonder if the inward heat of the body is cooled by draughts from the stream, for the flame is fed or fails according to the fuel. As hay, straw, wood, oil, and such like things are the nourishment which feeds fire, if you take them away, or do not supply them, the fire is extinguished. In like manner then the heat of the body is supported or lessened by food, it is excited by food and lessened by food. Luxury then is the mother of lust.

27. And is not temperance agreeable to nature, and to that divine law, which in the very beginning of all created things gave the springs for drink and the fruits of the trees for food? After the Flood the just man found wine a source of temptation to him. Genesis 9:20 Let us then use the natural drink of temperance, and would that we all were able to do so. But because all are not strong the Apostle said: Use a little wine because of your frequent infirmities. 1 Timothy 5:23 We must drink it then not for the sake of pleasure, but because of infirmity, and therefore sparingly as a remedy, not in excess as a gratification.

28. Lastly, Elijah, whom the Lord was training to the perfection of virtue, found at his head a cake and a cruse of water; and then fasted in the strength of that food forty days and forty nights. Our fathers, when they passed across the sea on foot, Exodus 17:6 drank water not wine. Daniel and the Hebrew children, fed with their peculiar food, Daniel 1:8 and with water to drink, overcame, the former the fury of the lions; Daniel 6:22 the latter saw the burning fire play around their limbs with harmless touch. Daniel 3:27

29. And why should I speak of men? Judith, in no way moved by the luxurious banquet of Holophernes, carried off the triumph of which men's arms despaired, solely in right of her temperance; delivered her country from occupation and slew the leader of the expedition with her own hands. A clear proof both that his luxury had enervated that warrior, terrible to the nations, and that temperance made this woman stronger than men. In this case it was not in her sex that nature was surpassed, but she overcame by her diet. Esther by her fasts moved a proud king. Esther 4:16 Anna, who for eighty-four years in her widowhood had served God with fasts and prayers day and night in the temple, Luke 2:37 recognized Christ, Whom John, the master of abstinence, and as it were a new angel on earth, announced.

30. O foolish Elisha, for feeding the prophets with wild and bitter gourds! O Ezra forgetful of Scripture, though he did restore the Scriptures from memory! Ezra 7:6 foolish Paul, who glories in fastings, 2 Corinthians 11:27 if fastings profit nothing.

31. But how should that not be profitable by which our sins are purged? And if you offer this with humility and with mercy, your bones, as Isaiah said, shall be

fat, and you shall be like a well-watered garden. Isaiah 58:11 So, then, your soul shall grow fat and its virtues also by the spiritual richness of fasting, and your fruits shall be multiplied by the fertility of your mind, so that there may be in you the inebriation of soberness, like that cup of which the Prophet says: Your cup which inebriates, how excellent it is!

32. But not only is that temperance worthy of praise which moderates food, but also that which moderates lust. Since it is written: Go not after your lusts, and deny your appetite. If you give her desires to your soul, you will be a joy to your enemies; Sirach 18:30-31 and farther on; Wine and women make even wise men to fall away. Sirach 19:2 So that Paul teaches temperance even in marriage itself; for he who is incontinent in marriage is a kind of adulterer, and violates the law of the Apostle.

33. And why should I tell how great is the grace of virginity, which was found worthy to be chosen by Christ, that it might be even the bodily temple of God, in which as we read the fullness of the Godhead dwelt bodily. Colossians 2:9 A Virgin conceived the Salvation of the world, a Virgin brought forth the life of all. Virginity then ought not to be left to itself, seeing that it benefited all in Christ. A Virgin bore Him Whom this world cannot contain or support. And when He was born from His mother's womb, He yet preserved the fence of her chastity and the inviolate seal of her virginity. And so Christ found in the Virgin that which He willed to make His own, that which the Lord of all might take to Himself. Further, our flesh was cast out of Paradise by a man and woman and was joined to God through a Virgin.

34. What shall I say concerning the other Mary, the sister of Moses, who as leader of the women passed on foot the straits of the sea? Exodus 15:20 By the same gift Thecla also was reverenced by the lions, so that the unfed beasts stretched at the feet of their prey prolonged a holy fast, and harmed the virgin neither with wanton look nor claw, since virginity is injured even by a look.

35. Again, with what reverence for virginity has the holy Apostle spoken: Concerning virgins I have no commandment of the Lord, but I give my counsel, as having obtained mercy of the Lord. 1 Corinthians 7:25 He has received no commandment, but a counsel, for that which beyond the law is not commanded, but is rather advised by way of counsel. Authority is not assumed but grace is shown, and this is not shown by anyone, but by him who obtained mercy from the Lord. Are then the counsels of these men better than those of the apostles? The Apostle says, I give my counsel, but they think it right to dissuade any from cultivating virginity.

36. And we ought to recognize what commendation of it the prophet, or rather Christ in the prophet, has uttered in a short verse; A garden enclosed, says He, is My sister, My spouse, a garden enclosed, a sealed fountain. Song of Songs 4:12 Christ says this to the Church, which he desires to be a virgin, without spot, without a wrinkle. A fertile garden is virginity, which can bear many fruits of good odour. A garden enclosed, because it is everywhere shut in by the wall of chastity. A sealed fountain, because virginity is the source and origin of modesty, having to

keep inviolate the seal of purity, in which source the image of God is reflected, since the purity of simplicity agrees also with chastity of the body.

37. And no one can doubt that the Church is a virgin, who also in the Epistle to the Corinthians is espoused and presented as a chaste virgin to Christ.
2 Corinthians 11:2 So in the first Epistle he gives his counsel, and esteems the gift of virginity as good, since it is not disturbed by any troubles of the present time, nor polluted by any of its defilements, nor shaken by any storms; in the later Epistle he brings a spouse to Christ, because he is able to certify the virginity of the Church in the purity of that people.

38. Answer me now, O Paul, in what way you give counsel for the present distress. 1 Corinthians 7:26 Because he that is without a wife is careful, he says, for the things of the Lord, how he may please God. And he adds, The unmarried woman and the virgin think of the things of the Lord, that they may be holy in body and spirit. 1 Corinthians 7:32 She has then her wall against the tempests of this world, and so fortified by the defense of divine protection she is disturbed by none of the blasts of this world. Good then is counsel, because there is advantage in counsel, but there is a bond in a commandment. Counsel attracts the willing, commandment binds the unwilling. If then anyone has followed counsel, and not repented, she has gained an advantage; but if she has repented, she has no ground for blaming the Apostle, for she ought herself to have judged of her own weakness; and so she is responsible for her own will, inasmuch as she bound herself by a bond and knot beyond her power to bear.

39. And so like a good physician, desiring to preserve the stability of virtue in the strong, and to give health to the weak, he gives counsel to the one, and points out the remedy to the others: He that is weak eats herbs, Romans 14:2 let him take a wife; he that has more power let him seek the stronger meat of virtue. And rightly he added: For he who being steadfast has settled in his own heart, having no necessity, but has power over his own will, and has determined this in his own heart, to keep his own virgin, does well. So then both he who gives his own virgin in marriage, does well; and he that gives her not in marriage, does better. A woman is bound by the law, for so long a time as her husband lives. But if her husband have fallen asleep, she is freed, let her marry whom she will, only in the Lord. But she will be more happy if she abide as she is, after my counsel, for I think that I also have the Spirit of the Lord. 1 Corinthians 7:37-40 This is to have the counsel of God, to search diligently into all things, and to advise things that are best, and to point out those that are safest.

40. A careful guide points out many paths, that each may walk along the one which he prefers and considers suitable to himself, so long as he comes upon one by which he can reach the camp. The path of virginity is good, but being high and steep requires the stronger wayfarers. Good also is that of widowhood, not so difficult as the former, but being rocky and rough, it requires more cautious travellers. Good too is that of marriage; being smooth and even it reaches the camp of the saints by a longer circuit. This way is taken by most. There are then the rewards of virginity, there are the merits of widowhood, there is also a place for conjugal modesty. There are steps and advances in each and every virtue.

41. Stand therefore firm in your hearts, that no one overthrow you, that no one be able to make you fall. The Apostle has taught us what it is to stand, that is what was said to Moses: The place whereon you stand is holy ground; Exodus 3:5 for no one stands unless he stand by faith, unless he stands fixed in the determination of his own heart. In another place also we read: But stand here with Me. Each sentence was spoken by the Lord to Moses, both Where you stand is holy ground, and Stand here with Me, that is, you stand with Me, if you stand firm in the Church. For the very place is holy, the very ground is fruitful with sanctity and fertile with harvests of virtues.

42. Stand then in the Church, stand where I appeared to you, where I am with you. Where the Church is, there is the most solid resting place for your mind, there the support of your soul, where I appeared to you in the bush. You are the bush, I am the fire; the fire in the bush, I in the flesh. Therefore am I the fire, that I may give light to you, that I may consume your thorns, that is, your sins, and show you My grace.

43. Standing firm then in your hearts, drive away from the Church the wolves which seek to carry off prey. Let there be no sloth in you, let not your mouth be evil nor your tongue bitter. Do not sit in the council of vanity; for it is written, I have not sat in the council of vanity. Do not listen to those who speak against their neighbours, lest while you listen to others, you be stirred up yourselves to speak against your neighbours, and it be said to each of you: You sat and spoke against your brother.

44. Men sit when speaking against others, they stand when they praise the Lord, to whom it is said: Behold now, praise the Lord, all you servants of the Lord, you that stand in the house of the Lord. He who sits, to speak of the bodily habit, is as it were loosened by ease, and relaxes the energy of his mind. But the careful watchman, the active searcher, the watchful guardian, who keeps the outposts of the camp, stands. The zealous warrior, too, who desires to anticipate the designs of the enemy, stands in array before he is expected.

45. Let him that stands take heed lest he fall. 1 Corinthians 10:12 He who stands does not give way to detraction, for it is the tales of those at ease in which detraction is spread abroad, and malignity betrayed. So that the prophet says: I have hated the congregation of the malignant, and will not sit with the ungodly. And in the thirty-sixth Psalm, which he has filled with moral precepts, he has put at the very beginning: Be not malignant among the malignant, neither be envious of those who do iniquity. Malignancy is more harmful than malice, because malignancy has neither pure simplicity nor open malice, but a hidden ill-will. And it is more difficult to guard against what is hidden than against what is known. For which reason too our Saviour warns us to beware of malignant spirits, because they would catch us by the appearance of sweet pleasures and a show of other things, when they hold forth honour to entice us to ambition, riches to avarice, power to pride.

46. And so both in every action, and especially in the demand for a bishop, by whom [as a pattern] the life of all is formed; malignity ought to be absent; so that

the man who is to be elected out of all, and to heal all, may be preferred to all by a calm and peaceful decision. For the meek man is the physician of the heart. And the Lord in the Gospel called Himself this, when He said: They that be whole need not a physician, but they that are sick. Matthew 9:12

47. He is the good Physician, Who has taken upon Him our infirmities, has healed our sicknesses, and yet He, as it is written, honoured not Himself to be made a High Priest, but He Who spoke to Him. The Father said: You are My Son, this day have I begotten You. Hebrews 5:5 As He said in another place: You are a Priest for ever after the order of Melchisedech. Who, since He was the type of all future priests, took our flesh upon Him, that in the days of His flesh He might offer prayers and supplications with a loud voice and tears; and by those things which He suffered, though He was the Son of God, might seem to learn obedience, which He taught us, that He might be made to us the Author of Salvation. And at last when His sufferings were completed, as though completed and made perfect Himself, He gave health to all, He bore the sin of all.

48. And so He Himself also chose Aaron as priest, that not the will of man but the grace of God should have the chief part in the election of the priest; Numbers 16:40 not the voluntary offering of himself, nor the taking it upon himself, but the vocation from heaven, that he should offer gifts for sins who could be touched for those who sinned, for He Himself, it is said, bears our weakness. Hebrews 5:2 No one ought to take this honour upon himself but they are called of God, as was Aaron, Hebrews 5:4 and so Christ did not demand but received the priesthood.

49. Lastly, when the succession derived through family descent from Aaron, contained rather heirs of the family than sharers in his righteousness, there came, after the likeness of that Melchisedech, of whom we read in the Old Testament, the true Melchisedech, the true King of peace, the true King of righteousness, for this is the interpretation of the Name, without father, without mother, without genealogy, having neither beginning of days nor end of life, Hebrews 5:3 which also refers to the Son of God, Who in His Divine Generation had no mother, was in His Birth of the Virgin Mary without a father; begotten before the ages of the Father alone, born in this age of the Virgin alone, and certainly could have no beginning of days seeing He was in the beginning. John 1:1 And how could He have any end of life, Who is the Author of life to all? He is the Beginning and the Ending. Revelation 1:8 But this also is referred to Him as an example, that a priest ought to be without father and without mother, since in him it is not nobility of family, but holiness of character and pre-eminence in virtue which is elected.

50. Let there be in him faith and ripeness of character, not one without the other, but let both meet together in one with good works and deeds. For which reason the Apostle Paul wishes that we should be imitators of them, who, as he says, by faith and patience Hebrews 6:12 possess the promises made to Abraham, who by patience was found worthy to receive and to possess the grace of the blessing promised to him. David the prophet warns us that we should be imitators of holy Aaron, and has set him among the Saints of God to be imitated by us, saying:

Moses and Aaron among his priests, and Samuel among those that call upon His Name.

51. A man clearly worthy to be proposed that all should follow him was he, for when a terrible death on account of the rebels was spreading over the people, he offered himself between the dead and the living, that he might arrest death, and that no more should perish. Numbers 16:48 A man truly of priestly mind and soul, who as a good shepherd with pious affection offered himself for the Lord's flock. And so he broke the sting of death, restrained its violence, refused it further course. Affection aided his deserts, for he offered himself for those who were resisting him.

52. Let those then who dissent learn to fear to rouse up the Lord, and to appease His priests. What! Did not the earthquake swallow up Dathan, Abiron, and Korah because of their dissension? Numbers 16:32 For when Korah, Dathan, and Abiron had stirred up two hundred and fifty men against Moses and Aaron to separate themselves from them, they rose up against them and said: Let it suffice you that all the congregation are holy, every one, and the Lord is among them. Numbers 16:3

53. Whereupon the Lord was angry and spoke to the whole congregation. The Lord considered and knew those that were His, and drew His saints to Himself; and those whom He chose not, He did not draw to Himself. And the Lord commanded that Korah and all those who had risen up with him against Moses and Aaron the priests of the Lord should take to themselves censers, and put on incense, Numbers 16:17 that he who was chosen of the Lord might be established as holy among the Levites of the Lord.

54. And Moses said to Korah: Hear me, you sons of Levi: Is this a small thing unto you, that God has separated you from the congregation of Israel, and brought you near to Himself, to minister the service of the Tabernacle of the Lord. Numbers 16:8-9 And farther on, Seek the priesthood also, so that you and all your congregation are gathered against the Lord. And what is Aaron that you murmur about him? Numbers 16:9-11

55. Considering, then, what causes of offense existed, that unworthy persons desired to discharge the offices of the priesthood, and therefore were causing dissensions; and were murmuring in censure of the judgment of God in the choice of His priest, the whole people were seized with a great fear, and dread of punishment came upon them all. But when all implore that all perish not for the insolence of few, those guilty of the wickedness are marked out; and two hundred and fifty men with their leaders are separated from the whole body of the people; and then the earth with a groan cleaves asunder in the midst of the people, a deep gulf opens, the offenders are swallowed up, and are so removed from all the elements of this world, as neither to pollute the air by breathing it, nor the heavens by beholding them, nor the sea by their touch, nor the earth by their sepulchres.

56. The punishment ceased, but the wickedness ceased not; for from this very thing a murmuring rose among them that the people had perished through the

priests. In His wrath at this, the Lord would have destroyed them all, had He not been moved first by the prayers of Moses and Aaron, and afterwards also at the intervention of His priest Aaron (the humiliation of their forgiveness being thereby greater), He willed to give their lives to those whose privilege they had repudiated.

57. Miriam the prophetess herself, who with her brothers had crossed the straits of the sea on foot, because, being still ignorant of the mystery of the Ethiopian woman, she had murmured against her brother Moses, broke out with leprous spots, Numbers 12:10 so that she would scarcely have been freed from so great a plague, unless Moses had prayed for her. Although this murmuring refers to the type of the Synagogue, which is ignorant of the mystery of that Ethiopian woman, that is the Church gathered out of the nations, and murmurs with daily reproaches, and envies that people through whose faith itself also shall be delivered from the leprosy of its unbelief, according to what we read that: blindness in part has happened unto Israel, until the fullness of the Gentiles be come in, and so all Israel shall be saved. Romans 11:25

58. And that we may observe that divine grace rather than human works in priests, of the many rods which Moses had received according to the Tribes, and had laid up, that of Aaron alone blossomed. And so the people saw that the gift of the Divine vocation is to be looked for in a priest, and ceased from claiming equal grace for a human choice though they had before thought that a similar prerogative belonged to themselves. But what else does that rod show, but that priestly grace never decays, and in the deepest lowliness has in its office the flower of the power committed to it, or that this also is refered to in mystery? Nor do we think that it was without a purpose that this took place near the end of the life of Aaron the priest. It seems to be shown that the ancient people, full of decay through the oldness of the long-continued unfaithfulness of the priests, being fashioned again in the last times to zeal in faith and devotion by the example of the Church, will again send forth with revived grace its flowers dead through so many ages.

59. But what does this signify, that after Aaron was dead, the Lord commanded, not the whole people, but Moses alone, who is among the priests, to clothe Aaron's son Eleazar with the priest's garments, except that we should understand that priest must consecrate priest, and himself clothe him with the vestments, that is, with priestly virtues; and then, if he has seen that nothing is wanting to him of the priestly garments, and that all things are perfect, should admit him to the sacred altars. For he who is to supplicate for the people ought to be chosen of God and approved by the priests, lest there be anything which might give serious offense in him whose office it is to intercede for the offenses of others. For the virtue of a priest must be of no ordinary kind, since he has to guard not only from nearness to greater faults, but even the very least. He must also be prompt to have pity, not recall a promise, restore the fallen, have sympathy with pain, preserve meekness, love piety, repel or keep down anger, must be as it were a trumpet to excite the people to devotion, or to soothe them to tranquillity.

60. It is an old saying: Accustom yourself to be consistent, that your life may set forth as it were a picture, always preserving the same representation which it has received. How can he be consistent who at one time is inflamed by anger, at

another blazes up with fierce indignation, whose face now burns, and now again is changed to paleness, varying and changing color every moment? But let it be so, let it be natural for one to be angry, or that there is generally a cause, it is a man's duty to restrain anger, and not to be carried away like a lion by fury, so as not to know to be quieted, not to spread tales, nor to embitter family quarrels; for it is written: A wrathful man digs up sin. Proverbs 15:18 He will not be consistent who is double-minded; he cannot be consistent who cannot restrain himself when angry, as to which David well says: Be angry and sin not. He does not govern his anger, but indulges his natural disposition, which a man cannot indeed prevent but may moderate. Therefore even though we are angry, let our passion admit only such emotion as is according to nature, not sin contrary to nature. For who would endure that he should not be able to govern himself, who has undertaken to govern others?

61. And so the Apostle has given a pattern, saying that a bishop must be blameless, 1 Timothy 3:2 and in another place: A bishop must be without offense, as a steward of God, not proud, not soon angry, not given to wine, not a striker, not greedy of filthy lucre. Titus 1:7 For how can the compassion of a dispenser of alms and the avarice of a covetous man agree together?

62. I have set down these things which I have been told are to be avoided, but the Apostle is the Master of virtues, and he teaches that gainsayers are to be convicted with patience, Titus 1:9 who lays down that one should be the husband of a single wife, Titus 1:6 not in order to exclude him from the right of marriage (for this is beyond the force of the precept), but that by conjugal chastity he may preserve the grace of his baptismal washing; nor again that he may be induced by the Apostle's authority to beget children in the priesthood; for he speaks of having children, not of begetting them, or marrying again.

63. And I have thought it well not to pass by this point, because many contend that having one wife is said of the time after Baptism; so that the fault whereby any obstacle would ensue would be washed away in baptism. And indeed all faults and sins are washed away; so that if anyone have polluted his body with very many whom he has bound to himself by no law of marriage, all the sins are forgiven him, but if any one have contracted a second marriage it is not done away; for sin not law is loosed by the laver, and as to baptism there is no sin but law. That then which has to do with law is not remitted as though it were sin, but is retained. And the Apostle has established a law, saying: If any man be without reproach the husband of one wife. 1 Timothy 3:2 So then he who is without blame the husband of one wife comes within the rule for undertaking the priestly office; he, however, who has married again has no guilt of pollution, but is disqualified for the priestly prerogative.

64. We have stated what is according to the law, let us state in addition what is according to reason. But first we must notice that not only has the Apostle laid down this rule concerning a bishop or priest, but that the Fathers in the Nicene Council added that no one who has contracted a second marriage ought to be admitted among the clergy at all. For how can he comfort or honour a widow, or exhort her to preserve her widowhood, and the faith pledged to her husband, which

he himself has not kept in regard to his former marriage? Or what difference would there be between people and priest, if they were bound by the same laws? The life of a priest ought to excel that of others as does his grace, for he who binds others by his precepts ought himself to keep the precepts of the law.

65. How I resisted my ordination, and lastly, when I was compelled, endeavoured that it might at least be deferred, but the prescribed rule did not prevail against the popular eagerness. Yet the Western Bishops approved of my ordination by their decision, the Eastern by an example of the same kind. And yet the ordination of a neophyte is forbidden, lest he should be lifted up by pride. 1 Timothy 3:6 If the ordination was not postponed it was because of constraint, and if humility suitable to the priestly office be not wanting, where there is no reason blame will not be imputed to him.

66. But if so much consideration is needed in other churches for the ordination of a bishop, how much care is required in the Church of Vercellæ, where two things seem to be equally required of the bishop, monastic rule and church discipline? For Eusebius of holy memory was the first in Western lands to bring together these differing matters, both while living in the city observing the rules of the monks, and ruling the Church with fasting and temperance. For the grace of the priesthood is much increased if the bishop constrain young men to the practice of abstinence, and to the rule of purity; and forbid them though living in the city, the manners and mode of life of the city.

67. From such a rule sprang those great men, Elijah, Elisha, John the son of Elizabeth, who clothed in sheepskins, poor and needy, and afflicted with pain, wandered in deserts, Hebrews 11:37 in hollows and thickets of mountains, among pathless rocks, rough caves, pitfalls and marshes, of whom the world was not worthy. From the same, Daniel, Ananias, Azarias, and Misael, Daniel 1:16 who were brought up in the royal palace, were fed meagrely as though in the desert, with coarse food, and ordinary drink. Rightly did those royal slaves prevail over kingdoms, despise captivity, shaking off its yoke, subdue powers, conquer the elements, quench the nature of fire, dull the flames, blunt the edge of the sword, stop the mouths of lions; Hebrews 11:33-34 they were found most strong when esteemed to be most weak, and did not shrink from the mockings of men, because they looked for heavenly rewards; they did not dread the darkness of the prison, on whom was shining the beauty of eternal light.

68. Following these, holy Eusebius went forth out of his country, and from his own relatives, and preferred a foreign wandering to ease at home. For the faith also he preferred and chose the hardships of exile, in conjunction with Dionysius of holy memory, who esteemed a voluntary exile above an Emperor's friendship. And so these illustrious men, surrounded with arms, closed in by soldiers, when torn away from the larger Church, triumphed over the imperial power, because by earthly shame they purchased fortitude of soul, and kingly power; they from whom the band of soldiers and the din of arms could not tear away the faith subdued the raging of the brutal mind, which was unable to hurt the saints. For, as you read in Proverbs, the king's wrath is as the wrath of a lion. Proverbs 19:12

69. He confessed that he was overcome when he asked them to change their determination, but they thought their pen stronger than swords of iron. Then it was unbelief which was wounded so that it fell, not the faith of the saints; they did not desire a tomb in their own country, for whom was reserved a home in the heavens. They wandered over the whole earth, having nothing and yet possessing all things. 2 Corinthians 6:10 Wherever they were sent, they esteemed it a place full of delights, for nothing was wanting to them in whom the riches of faith abounded. Lastly, they enriched others, being themselves poor as to earthly means, rich in grace. They were tried but not killed, in fasting, in labours, in watchings, in vigils. Out of weakness they came forth strong. They did not wait for the enticements of pleasure who were satiated by fasting; the burning summer did not parch those whom the hope of eternal grace refreshed, nor did the cold of icy regions break them down, whose devotion was ever budding afresh with glowing devotion; they feared not the chains of men whom Jesus had set free; they desired not to be rescued from death, who expected to be raised again by Christ.

70. And at last holy Dionysius requested in his prayers, that he might end his life in exile, for fear that he might, if he returned home, find the minds of the people or the clergy disturbed through the teaching or practice of the unbelievers, and he obtained this favour, so that he bore with him the peace of the Lord with a quiet mind. Thus as holy Eusebius first raised the standard of confessorship, so blessed Dionysius in his exile gave up his life with honour higher even than martyrs.

71. Now this patience in holy Eusebius grew strong by the discipline of the monastery, and from the custom of hard endurance he derived the power of enduring hardships. For who doubts that in stricter Christian devotion these two things are the most excellent, the offices of the clergy and the rule of the monks? The former is a discipline which accustoms to courteousness and good morals, the latter to abstinence and patience; the former as it were on an open stage, the latter in secret; the one is visible, the other hidden. And so he who was a good athlete said: We are made a spectacle to this world and to Angels. 1 Corinthians 6:9 Worthy indeed was he to be gazed upon by Angels, when he was striving to attain the prize of Christ, when he was striving to lead on earth the life of Angels, and overcome the wickedness of spirits in heaven, for he wrestled with spiritual wickedness. Ephesians 6:12 Rightly did the world gaze upon him, that it might imitate him.

72. The one life, then, is on the open arena, the other hidden as in a cave; the one is opposed to the confusion of the world, the other to the desires of the flesh; the one subdues, the other shuns the pleasures of the body; the one was more agreeable, the other more safe; the one ruling, the other restraining itself, in order to be wholly Christ's, for to the perfect it is said: He who will come after Me, let him deny himself, and take up his cross and follow Me. Matthew 17:24 Now he follows Christ who is able to say: It is no longer I that live, but Christ lives in me. Galatians 2:20

73. Paul denied himself, when, knowing that chains and tribulations awaited him in Jerusalem, he willingly offered himself to danger, saying: Nor do I count my life dear to myself, if only I can accomplish my course, and the ministry of the

Word, which I have received of the Lord Jesus. Acts 20:24 And at last, though many were standing round, weeping and beseeching him, he did not change his mind, so stern a censor of itself is ready faith.

74. The one then contends, the other retires; the one overcomes incitements, the other flees from them; by the one the world is triumphed over, the other rejoices over it; to the one the world is crucified, or itself is crucified to the world, Galatians 6:14 to the other it is unknown; the one endures more frequent temptations, and so has the greater victory, the other falls less often, and keeps guard more easily.

75. Elijah himself too, that the word spoken by his mouth might be confirmed, was sent by the Lord to hide himself by the brook Cherith. Ahab threatened, Jezebel threatened, Elijah was afraid and rose up, and then went in the strength of that spiritual meat forty days and forty nights unto Horeb the mount of God; and entered into a cave and rested there; and afterwards was sent to anoint kings. He was then inured to patience by dwelling in solitude, and, as though fed to the fatness of virtue by the homely food, went on more strong.

76. John, too, grew up in the desert, and baptized the Lord, and there first practised constancy, that afterwards he might rebuke kings.

77. And since in speaking of holy Elijah's dwelling in the desert, we have passed by without notice the names of places which were not given without a purpose, it seems well to go back to what they signify. Elijah was sent to the brook Cherith, and there the ravens nourished him, bringing him bread in the morning, for it strengthens man's heart. For how should the prophet be nourished except by mystical food? At evening flesh was supplied. Understand what you read, for Cherith means understanding, Horeb signifies heart or as a heart, Beersheba also is interpreted the well of the seventh, or of the oath.

78. Elijah went first to Beersheba, to the mysteries and sacraments of the divine and holy Law, next he is sent to the brook, to the stream of the river which makes glad the City of God. You perceive the two Testaments of the One Author; the old Scripture as a well deep and obscure, whence you can only draw with labour; it is not full, for He Who was to fill it was not yet come, Who afterwards said: I have come not to destroy but to fulfil the Law. Matthew 5:17 And so the Saint is bidden of the Lord to pass over to the stream, for he who has drunk of the New Testament, not only is a river, but also from his belly shall flow rivers of living water, John 7:38 rivers of understanding, rivers of meditation, spiritual rivers, which, however, dried up in the times of unbelief, lest the sacrilegious and unbelieving should drink.

79. At that place the ravens recognized the Prophet of the Lord, whom the Jews did not recognize. The ravens fed him, whom that royal and noble race were persecuting. What is Jezebel, who persecuted him but the Synagogue, vainly fluent, vainly abounding in the Scriptures, which it neither keeps nor understands? What ravens fed him but those whose young call upon Him, to whose cattle He gives food as we read; to the young ravens that call upon Him. Those ravens knew

whom they were feeding, who were close upon understanding, and brought food to that stream of sacred knowledge.

80. He feeds the prophet, who understands and keeps the things that are written. Our faith gives him sustenance, our progress gives him nourishment; he feeds upon our minds and senses, his discourse is nourished by our understanding. In the morning we give him bread, who, being placed in the light of the Gospel, bestow on him the settled strength of our hearts. By these things he is nourished, by these he is strong, with these he fills the mouths of those who fast, to whom the unbelief of the Jews supplied no food of faith. To them every prophetic utterance is but fasting diet, the interior richness of which they do not see; empty and thin, such as cannot fatten their jaws.

81. Perhaps they brought him flesh in the evening, as it were stronger food, such as the Corinthians, whose minds were weak, could not take, and were therefore fed by the Apostle with milk. 1 Corinthians 3:2 So, stronger meat was brought in the evening of the world, in the morning bread. And so, because the Lord commanded this food to be supplied, that word of prophecy may be suitably addressed to Him in this place: You will give joy in the outgoings of morning and evening; and, farther on: You have prepared their food, for so is its preparation.

82. But I think that enough has been said of the Master, let us now go on to the lives of the disciples, who have given themselves to His praise and celebrate it with hymns day and night. For this is the service of the Angels, to be always occupied in the praises of God, to propitiate and entreat the Lord with frequent prayers. They attend to reading, or occupy their minds with continual labours, and separated from the companionship of women, afford safe protection to each other. What a life is this, in which is nothing to fear, much to imitate! The pain of fasting is compensated by tranquillity of mind, is lightened by practice, aided by leisure, or beguiled by occupation; is not burdened with worldly cares, nor occupied with uncongenial troubles, nor weighed down with the distractions of the city.

83. You perceive what kind of teacher must be found for the preservation or teaching of this gift, and we can find him, if you assist by unanimity, if you forgive one another should any one think himself injured by another. For it is not the only kind of justice, not to injure him who has not injured us, but also to forgive him who has most injured us. We are often injured by the fraud of another, by the guile of a neighbour; do we consider it a mark of virtue, to avenge guile by guile, or to repay fraud by fraud? For if justice is a virtue it should be free from offense, and should not repel wickedness by wickedness. For what virtue is it that the same thing should be done by you which you yourself punish in another? That is the spreading of wickedness not its punishment, for it makes no difference whom one injures, whether a just man or an unjust, seeing one ought not to injure anyone. Nor does it make any difference in what way one bears ill will, whether from a desire of revenging oneself, or from a wish to injure, since in neither case is ill will free from blame. For to bear ill will is the same thing as to be unjust, and so it is said to you: Bear not ill will among those that bear ill will, and emulate not those that do unrighteousness; and above; I have hated the congregation of them

that bear ill will. He clearly comprehends all and makes no exception, he lays hold of ill will and asks not the cause.

84. But what better pattern can there be than that of Divine justice? For the Son of God says: Love your enemies; Matthew 5:44 and again: Pray for those that persecute you and speak against you. Matthew 5:44 So far does He remove the desire of vengeance from the perfect that He commands charity towards those who injure them. And since He had said in the Old Testament: Vengeance is Mine, I will repay. Deuteronomy 32:35 He says in the Gospel, that we are to pray for those who have injured us, that He Who has said that He will avenge, may not do so; for it is His will to pardon at your desire with which according to His promise He agrees. But if you seek for you know that the unjust is more severely punished by his own convictions than by judicial severity.

85. And since no one can be without some adversities, let us take care that they do not happen to us through our own fault. For no one is more severely condemned by the judgment of others, than a foolish man, who is the cause of his misfortunes, is condemned by his own. For which reason we should decline matters which are full of trouble and contention, which have no advantage, but cause hindrances. Although we ought to take care not to have to repent our decisions or acts. For it is the part of a prudent man to look forward, so as not often to have to repent, for never to repent belongs to God alone. But what is the fruit of righteousness, but tranquillity of mind? Or what is to live righteously but to live with tranquility? Such as is the pattern of the master, such is the condition of the whole house. But if these things are requisite in a house, how much more in the Church, where we, both rich and poor, bond and free, Greek and Scythian, noble and common, are all one in Christ Jesus. Colossians 3:11

86. Let no man suppose that because he is rich, more deference is to be paid him. In the Church he is rich who is rich in faith, for the faithful has a whole world of riches. What wonder is it if the faithful possesses the world, who possesses the inheritance of Christ, which is of more value than the world? You were redeemed with the Precious Blood, 1 Peter 1:18-19 was certainly said to all, not to the rich only. But if you will be rich, obey him who says: Be holy in all your conversation. 1 Peter 1:15 He is speaking not to the rich only but to all; for He judges without respect of persons, as the Apostle His faithful witness says. And therefore says he: Spend the time of your sojourning here, 1 Peter 1:17 not in luxury, or fastidiousness, nor haughtiness of heart, but in fear. On this earth you have time not eternity, do you use the time as those who must pass hence.

87. Do not trust in riches; for all such things are left here, faith alone will accompany you. And righteousness indeed will go with you if faith has led the way. Why do riches entice you? You were not redeemed with gold and silver, with possessions, or silk garments, from your vain conversation, but with the precious Blood of Christ. 1 Peter 1:18 He then is rich who is an heir of God, a joint heir with Christ. Despise not the poor man, he has made you rich. This poor man cried, and the Lord heard him. Do not reject a poor man, Christ when He was rich became poor, and became poor because of you, that by His poverty He might

make you rich. 2 Corinthians 8:9 Do not then as though rich exalt yourself, He sent forth His apostles without money.

88. And the first of them said: Silver and gold have I none. Acts 3:6 He glories in poverty as though shunning contamination. Silver and gold, he says, I have none,— not gold and silver. He knows not their order in value who knows not the use of them. Silver and gold have I none, but I have faith. I am rich enough in the Name of Jesus, which is above every name. Philippians 2:9 I have no silver, neither do I require any; I have no gold, neither do I desire it, but I have what you rich men have not, I have what even you would consider to be of more value, and I give it to the poor, namely that I say in the Name of Jesus: Be strengthened, you weak hands, and you feeble knees. Isaiah 35:3

89. But if you will be rich, you must be poor. Then shall you in all things be rich, if you are poor in spirit. It is not property which makes rich, but the spirit.

90. There are those who humble themselves in abundance of riches, and they act rightly and prudently, for the law of nature is sufficiently rich for all, according to which one may soon find what is more than enough; but for lust any abundance of riches is still penury. Again, no one is born poor but becomes so. Poverty then is not in nature but in our own feelings, and so to find oneself rich is easy for nature, but hard for lust. For the more a man has gained the more he thirsts for gain, and burns as it were with a kind of intoxication from his lusts.

91. Why do you seek for a heap of riches as though it were necessary? Nothing is so necessary as to know that this is not necessary. Why do you throw the blame on the flesh? It is not the belly in the body but avarice in the mind which makes a man insatiable. Does the flesh take away the hope of the future? Does the flesh destroy the sweetness of spiritual grace? Does the flesh hinder faith? Is it the flesh which attributes any weight to vain opinions as it were to insane masters? The flesh prefers frugal moderation, by which it is freed from burdens, is clothed with health, because it has laid aside its care and has obtained tranquillity.

92. But riches themselves are not blameable. For the ransom of a man's life are his riches, Proverbs 13:8 since he that gives to the poor redeems his soul. So that even in these material riches there is place for virtue. You are like steersmen in the vast sea. If a man steers his course well, he quickly passes over the sea so as to attain to the port, but one who knows not how to direct his property is drowned together with his freight. And so it is written: The wealth of rich men is a most strong city. Proverbs 10:15

93. And what is that city but Jerusalem which is in heaven, in which is the kingdom of God? This is a good possession which brings eternal fruit. A good possession which is not left here, but is possessed there. He who possesses this says: The Lord is my portion. He says not, My portion stretches and extends from this boundary to that. Nor does he say, My portion is among such and such neighbours, except perchance among the apostles, among the prophets, among the saints of the Lord, for this is the righteous man's portion. He does not say, My portion is in the meadows, or in the woods, or the plains, except perchance those

wooded plains in which the Church is found, of which it is written: We found it in the wooded plains. He does not say, My portion consists of herds of horses, for a horse is a vain thing for safety. He does not say, My portion consists of herds of oxen, asses, or sheep; except perchance he reckons himself among those which know their Owner, and wishes to company with the ass which does not shun the crib Isaiah 1:3 of Christ; and that Sheep is his portion which was led to the slaughter, and that Lamb which was dumb before the shearer, and opened not His mouth, Isaiah 53:7 in Whose humiliation judgment has been exalted. Well does he say before the shearer, for He laid aside what was additional, not His own essence, on the cross, when He laid aside His Body, but lost not His Divinity.

94. It is not then everyone who can say, The Lord is my portion. The covetous man cannot, for covetousness draws near and says: You are my portion, I have you in subjection, you have served me, you have sold yourself to me with that gold, by that possession you have adjudged yourself to me. The luxurious man says not: Christ is my portion, for luxury comes and says: You are my portion, I made you mine in that banquet, I caught you in the net of that feast, I hold you by the bond of your gluttony. Do you not know that your table was more valued by you than your life? I refute you by your own judgment, deny if you can, but you can not. And in fine you have reserved nothing for your life, you have spent it all for your table. The adulterer cannot say: The Lord is my portion; for lust comes and says: I am your portion, you bound yourself to me in the love of that maiden, by a night with that harlot you have come under my laws and into my power. The traitor cannot say: Christ is my portion, for at once the wickedness of his sin rushes on him and says: He is deceiving You, Lord Jesus, he is mine.

95. We have an example of this, for when Judas had received the bread from Christ the devil entered into his heart, as though claiming his own property, as though retaining his right to his own portion, as though saying: He is not Yours but mine; clearly he is my servant, Your betrayer, plainly he is mine. He sits at table with You, and serves me; with You he feasts, but is fed by me; from You he receives bread, from me money; with You he drinks, and has sold Your Blood to me. And he proved how truly he spoke. Then Christ departed from him, Judas also himself left Jesus and followed the devil.

96. How many masters has he who has forsaken the One! But let us not forsake Him. Who would forsake Him Whom they follow bound with chains indeed, but chains of love, which set free and do not bind, those chains in which they who are bound boast, saying: Paul the bondservant of Jesus Christ, and Timothy. Philippians 1:1 It is more glorious for us to be bound by Him, than to be set free and loosed from others. Who then would flee from peace? Who would flee from salvation? Who would flee from mercy? Who would flee from redemption?

97. You see, my sons, what has been the end of those who followed these things, how being dead they yet work. Let us study to gain the diligence of those the glory of whose virtues we admire, and what we praise in others, let us silently recognize in ourselves. Nothing effeminate, nothing feeble attains to praise. The kingdom of heaven suffers violence, and the violent take it by force. Matthew 11:12 The fathers ate the lamb in haste. Faith hastens, devotion is quick, hope is active, it

loves not objections of the mind, but to pass from fruitless ease to the fruits of toil. Why do you put off till tomorrow? You can gain today; and must guard against not attaining the one and losing the other. The loss even of one hour is no slight one, one hour is a portion of our whole life.

98. There are young persons who desire quickly to attain to old age, so as no longer to be subject to the will of their elders; and there are also old men who would wish if they could to return again to youth. And I approve of neither desire, for the young, disdainful of things present, as it were ungratefully desire a change in their way of living, the old wish for its lengthening, whereas youth can grow old in character, and old age grow green with action. For it is discipline as much as age which brings amendment of character. How much the more then ought we to raise our hopes to the kingdom of God, where will be newness of life, and where will be a change of grace not of age!

99. Reward is not obtained by ease or by sleep. The sleeper does no work, ease brings no profit, but rather loss. Esau by taking his ease lost the blessing of the first-born, for he preferred to have food given to him rather than to seek it. Industrious Jacob found favour with each parent.

100. And yet although Jacob was superior in virtue and favour, he yielded to his brother's anger, who grieved that his younger brother was preferred to him. And so it is written: Give place to wrath, Romans 12:19 lest the wrath of another draw you also into sin, when you wish to resist, and to avenge yourself. You can put away sin both from him and from yourself, if you think well to yield. Imitate the patriarch who by his mother's counsel went far away. And who was the mother? Rebecca, that is, Patience. For who but Patience could have given this counsel? The mother loved her son, but preferred that he should be cut off from herself rather than from God. And so because the mother was good, she benefited both her sons, but to the youngest she gave a blessing which he could keep; yet she preferred not one son to the other as sons; but the active to the easy-going, the faithful to the unbelieving.

101. And so since he was separated from his parents through piety not on account of impiety, he talked with God, he increased in riches, in children, and in favour. Nor was he elated by these things when he met his brother; but humbly bowed down to him, not indeed considering him the pitiless, the furious, the degenerate, but Him Whom he reverenced in him. And so he bowed down seven times, which is the number of remission, for he was not bowing down to man, but to Him Whom he foresaw in the Spirit, as hereafter to come in human flesh to take away the sins of the world. John 1:29 And this mystery is unfolded to you in the answer given to Peter, when he said: If my brother trespass against me how often shall I forgive him? Until seven times? Matthew 18:21 You see that remission of sins is a type of that great Sabbath, of that rest of everlasting grace, and therefore is given by contemplation.

102. But what is the meaning of his having arranged his wives and children and all his servants, and ordered that they should bow down to the earth? It was certainly not to the element of earth, which is often filled with blood, in which is the

workshop of all crimes, which often is rough with huge rocks, or broken cliffs, or barren and hungry soil, but as to that Flesh which is to be for our salvation. And perchance this is that mystery which the Lord taught, when He said: Not only seven times, but even seventy times seven. Matthew 18:22

103. Do you then forgive injuries done to you that you may be children of Jacob. Be not provoked as was Esau. Imitate holy David, who as a good master left us what we should follow, saying: Instead of loving me they spoke against me, but I prayed, and when he was reviled, he prayed. Prayer is a good shield, wherewith contumely is kept away, cursing is repelled and often is turned back on those who utter it, so that they are wounded by their own weapons. Let them curse, he says, but bless You. The curse of man is to be sought for, which procures the blessing of the Lord.

104. And for the rest, most dear brethren, consider that Jesus suffered without the gate, and do you go forth out of this earthly city, for your city is Jerusalem which is above. Let your conversation be there, that you may say: But our conversation is in heaven. Philippians 3:20 Therefore did Jesus go forth out of the city, that you going out of this world may be above the world. Moses alone, who saw God, had his tabernacle without the camp when he talked with God; Exodus 33:7 and the blood indeed of the victims which were offered for sin, was brought to the altar, but the bodies were burnt without the camp; Exodus 29:12-13 for no one placed amidst the evil of this world can lay aside sin, nor is his blood accepted of God, except he go forth from the defilement of this body.

105. Love hospitality, whereby holy Abraham found favour, and received Christ as his , and Sarah already worn with age gained a son; Lot also escaped the fire of the destruction of Sodom. You too can receive Angels if you offer hospitality to strangers. What shall I say of Rahab who by this means found safety?

106. Compassionate those who are bound with chains, as though bound with them. Comfort those in sorrow; for, It is better to go into the house of mourning than into the house of rejoicing. Ecclesiastes 7:2 From the one is gained the merit of a good work, from the other a lapse into sin. Lastly, in the one case you still hope for the reward, in the other you have already received it. Feel with those who are afflicted as if also afflicted with them.

107. Let a wife show deference, not be a slave to her husband; let her show herself ready to be ruled not coerced. She is not worthy of wedlock who deserves chiding. Let a husband also guide his wife like a steersman, honour her as the partner of his life, share with her as a joint heir of grace.

108. Mothers, wean your children, love them, but pray for them that they may long live above this earth, not on the earth but above it, for there is nothing long-lived on this earth, and that which lasts long is but short and very frail. Warn them rather to take up the Cross of the Lord than to love this life.

109. Mary, the mother of the Lord stood by her Son's Cross; no one has taught me this but the holy Evangelist St. John. John 19:25 Others have related how the earth

was shaken at the Lord's passion, the sky was covered with darkness, the sun withdrew itself; Matthew 27:45 that the thief was after a faithful confession received into paradise. Luke 23:43 John tells us what the others have not told, how the Lord fixed on the Cross called to His mother, esteeming it of more worth that, victorious over His sufferings, He rendered her the offices of piety, than that He gave her a heavenly kingdom. For if it be according to religion to grant pardon to the thief, it is a mark of much greater piety that a mother is honoured with such affection by her Son. Behold, He says, your Son....Behold your mother. John 19:27 Christ testified from the Cross, and divided the offices of piety between the mother and the disciple. The Lord made not only a public but also a private testament, and John signed this testament of His, a witness worthy of so great a Testator. A good testament not of money but of eternal life, which was written not with ink but with the Spirit of the living God, Who says: My tongue is the pen of a quickly writing scribe.

110. Nor was Mary below what was becoming the mother of Christ. When the apostles fled, she stood at the Cross, and with pious eyes beheld her Son's wounds, for she did not look for the death of her Offspring, but the salvation of the world. Or perchance, because that royal hall knew that the redemption of the world would be through the death of her Son, she thought that by her death also she might add something to the public good. But Jesus did not need a helper for the redemption of all, Who saved all without a helper. Wherefore also He says: I have become like a man without help, free among the dead. He received indeed the affection of His mother, but sought not another's help.

111. Imitate her, holy mothers, who in her only dearly beloved Son set forth so great an example of maternal virtue; for neither have you sweeter children, nor did the Virgin seek the consolation of being able to bear another son.

112. Masters, command your servants not as being below you in rank, but as remembering that they are sharers of the same nature as yourselves. 1 Peter 2:18 Servants, serve your masters with good will, for each ought patiently to support that to which he is born, and be obedient not only to good but also to froward masters. For what thanks has your service if you zealously serve good masters? But if you thus serve the froward also you gain merit; for the free also have no reward, if when they transgress they are punished by the judges, but this is their merit to suffer without transgressing. And so you, if contemplating the Lord Jesus you serve even difficult masters with patience, will have your reward. Since the Lord Himself suffered, the just at the hand of the unjust, and by His wonderful patience nailed our sins to His Cross, that he who shall imitate Him may wash away his sins in His Blood.

113. In fine, turn all to the Lord Jesus. Let your enjoyment of this life be with a good conscience, your endurance of death with the hope of immortality, your assurance of the resurrection through the grace of Christ; let truth be with simplicity, faith with confidence, abstinence with holiness, industry with soberness, conversation with modesty, learning without vanity; let there be soberness of doctrine, faith without the intoxication of heresy. The grace of our Lord Jesus Christ be with you all. Amen.

STROMATA

www.ingramcontent.com/pod-product-compliance
Lightning Source LLC
Chambersburg PA
CBHW051009140626
46546CB00016B/1376